Eike von Savigny

# The Social Foundations of Meaning

Springer-Verlag Berlin Heidelberg New York
London Paris Tokyo

Prof. Dr. EIKE VON SAVIGNY
Universität Bielefeld
Abteilung Philosophie
Postfach 8640
D-4800 Bielefeld 1

ISBN 3-540-19006-6 Springer-Verlag Berlin Heidelberg New York
ISBN 0-387-19006-6 Springer-Verlag New York Berlin Heidelberg

© Springer-Verlag Berlin Heidelberg 1988
Printed in Germany

Offset printing: Druckhaus Beltz, Hemsbach/Bergstr. Bookbinding: J. Schäffer OHG, Grünstadt.
2126/3130-543210

# Table of Contents

## Chapter IV
Conventional utterance meaning

## Chapter V
Against intentionalism

## Chapter VI
The same case for sentence meaning: NIVEAU

## Chapter VII
Some results for sentence meaning

Epilogue

# Introductory summary

The present book attempts to elaborate a pretheoretical intuition about the concept of linguistic meaning as it is embedded in the description of certain complex forms of conventional behavior. The attempt consists of three parts: An analysis of the relevant conventional facts; independent of this special analysis, an analysis of conventional utterance meaning in terms of conventional facts; and independent of this special analysis, an analysis of sentence meaning in terms of conventional utterance meaning.

Chapter I describes the general idea. After distinguishing conventional meaning from natural meaning (§ 1) and from speaker's meaning (§ 2), conventional meaning is provisionally identified with the way in which an expression has to be understood (§ 3). This leads up to the conventional result principle (§ 4): Any utterance, by virtue of its meaning, takes conventional effects which are different for different utterance meanings; saying something consists in committing oneself to such conventional results. The divergence from intention − oriented approaches to meaning is illustrated by the difference in speculative ideas on language evolution which the intentionalist and the conventionalist approaches suggest respectively (§ 5), and by a picture which regards communication as an ongoing process of modifying situational roles which only secondarily permits a parasitic process of disclosing and grasping intentions (§ 6).

Chapter II establishes an adequate empirical interpretation for those conventional facts which are actually used for analyzing utterance meanings in the present study (§ 16). This interpretation rests, basically, on an empirical concept of a group's observing a rule which is adapted (§ 8) from Hart's concept of the existence of rules, in a slightly modified (§ 9) version; critiques of Hart's concept are shown to rest on confusions (§ 10). The fashionable alternative, viz. Lewis' concept of convention, is dismissed on the ground that if its requirements are taken in an empirically significant sense, having such conventions is beyond the reach of average human communities (§§ 12−14); a hidden motive for one of these requirements − common knowledge of conventions −, viz. the introduction of Gricean meaning via convention, is shown to be misdirected (§ 15).

Chapter III ostensively describes the approach to utterance meaning by way of demonstration, on an natural signalling system, how the hypothesis that a language is embedded in a conventional system is to be confirmed. Rules ascribing utterance meanings to certain ways of behavior under certain circumstances are taken to hold because this assumption explains deviations from otherwise valid background conventions. The function of the case study procedure is to establish the claim that such meaning — positing descriptions of conventional systems can be judged by their merits in a disciplined way, and chapter III is restricted to this purpose. (The whole of this first part of the case study is given in Appendix I.)

According to chapter IV, conventional results are paired off with utterance meanings by a function $\Lambda$; descriptions of conventional systems which attribute utterance meanings to ways of behavior do so in making use of $\Lambda$. If this use of $\Lambda$ is inevitable for describing a conventional system, i.e. if one cannot do without the assumption that some kinds of behavior have utterance meanings, then they have these utterance meanings and are, therefore, utterances (§§ 23, 24). This roundabout way of determining utterances and speakers is argued to follow the common pattern of inference to the best explanation (§ 25). From the analysis of utterance meaning, some conclusions are drawn: The repertoire of a language is not restricted, in any of the commonly suspected ways, by its stock of expressions (§ 26); we cannot rely on having a clear concept of language (§ 27); and the speech act of reference is so very theoretical that it appears more indeterminate the less theoretical decisions are remembered (§ 28).

The aim of chapter V is polemic; it attempts to discredit approaches to utterance meaning which make essential use of speaker's intentions. A basic intention on account of which to understand the character of constative utterances does not exist (§ 30). Gricean intentions do not matter where they are present, and they are unlikely to be present anyway (§ 31). What speakers mean and what they say, non — accidentally coincides to a large measure — normally, speakers say what they mean; however, the connection is empirical rather than conceptual (§ 32). Three possible explanations are offered for the temptation to attribute an unduely central role to speaker's intentions: where social institutions are intimately connected with intentional acitvities, there is always the danger of trying to explain the social via the intentional, even if the correct explanation is the other way around (§ 33). Secondly, there is a possible explanation from English language philosophizing, turning on an syntactical ambiguity of the expression 'the meaning of' (§ 34), and, lastly, one from the general linguistic convention which permits the speaker to authorize a given interpretation of his utterance (§ 35).

Taking up the case study procedure again, chapter VI proceeds to the task of describing systems of utterance meaning rules where the kinds of behavior performing which counts as utterances — the signs — are not interchangeable (§ 36). This is shown to require the introduction of new theoretical entities (over and above utterance meanings) which must be held responsible for any particular sign's special contribution to the different meanings of its utterances under various circumstances (§ 37). A theory which posits such "suitability markers" (as they are called provisionally) involves, even for the simple natural signalling system unter scrutiny, an analysis of the semantical notions of ambiguity, of the rudiments of negation, and of anaphora (§ 38). (The whole of this part of the case study is given in Appendix II.)

Chapter VII defends the idea that the theoretical entities analyzed in the last chapter are sentence meanings, because they are what independently utterable — even if structureless — signs contribute to the meanings of their utterances (§ 39). Sentence meanings are then defined as what the best description of a language has to attribute to its independently utterable signs in order to cover all utterance meanings which are possible in this language (§ 40); this enterprise is distinguished from semantic theories of sentence meaning (§ 41). It follows from the definition that sentence meanings are still more theoretical than utterance meanings and comparable to the meanings of utterance circumstances; the usual identification of utterances with sentence tokens is mistaken (§ 42). If the definition is accepted, then one can show (§ 43) that the meaning of a sentence cannot on intuitive grounds, or *a priori*, reductively be identified either with what is common to what speakers mean whenever they utter it, or with its use in the sense of illocutionary act potential, or with the proposition of all of its utterance meanings, or with its truth conditions.

Against the background of the picture, developed in the seven chapters, of different theoretical levels of language description, the epilogue sketches how things which go under the rubric of "rule of language" are distinguished from and related to each other.

I would like to express my thanks to the people whose critical and encouraging help accompanied the working out of first thoughts: To participants in some courses I gave at the University of Bielefeld, among them Matthias Althoff, Martina Herrmann, Rosemarie Rheinwald, Gabriela Ruhmann, Oliver Scholz, and Otto Wolff; and colleagues who discussed some topics with me, among them Jonathan Bennett, Günther Grewendorf, Irene Heim, Mark Helme, Teresa Jacobsen, Andreas Kemmerling, Lorenz Krüger, Wolfgang Spohn, and Bernhard Thöle. From the following books the present study profitted most: Gilbert Ryle's

*The Concept of Mind*, John L. Austin's *How to Do Things With Words*, Ludwig Wittgenstein's *Philosophical Investigations*, Herbert L.A. Hart's *The Concept of Law*, David K. Lewis' *Convention*, Stephen R. Schiffer's *Meaning*, and Jonathan Bennett's *Linguistic Behaviour*.

I thank the Deutsche Forschungsgemeinschaft for generous support of several research projects during the last years, the results of which have eventually contributed to the present book.

In preparing this manuscript, I have used material from articles which have formerly been published in *American Philosophical Quaterly*, *Analysis*, *Erkenntnis*, *Philosophical Studies*, *Ratio*, and *Contemporary Aspects of Philosophy* (ed. Gilbert Ryle, Oriel Press). As far as a permission is required, I thank the editors and publishers for granting it, and the others I thank for not requiring it.

Last but not least, thanks are due to Brigitte Drappa for her patience in typing her way through different stages of the manuscript, and to Michael Schneider for his careful preparation of the print form.

# Chapter I
## Conventional meaning: The pretheoretical intuition

### § 1 Conventional meaning vs. natural meaning

If we speak of meaning, be it the meaning of signs and utterances,[1] or of other things and events, or what not, we may have in mind at least two different kinds of meaning: conventional meaning and natural meaning. In the present book, we are interested in conventional meaning. Let us try to distinguish both by two sets of criteria:

*Natural signs, or indicators:*

The gathering of starlings means winter is coming.

Yellowish clouds mean snow.

If someone sees many eyes in a Rorschach test, this is a sign of paranoic tendencies.

The queen of clubs means an untimely death.

These signs may be called 'indicators'. It is an old observation that indicators indicate what they indicate because an empirical correlation holds between their occurrence and the occurrence of the thing, fact, event, feature, or ... indicated. The following four characteristics of indicators are linked with this fact:

(N1) An indicator cannot be used to indicate something unless it is discovered beforehand that it indicates the thing indicated. Psychologists have discovered that people who usually see eyes in Rorschach tests often have paranoic tendencies. Discovering what indicators indicate means discovering the empirical correlation between the indicator and the thing indicated.

(N2) There can be any number of indicators which nobody has ever used nor ever will use. Of course it is difficult to give examples; for to be able to give an example one has to discover a correlation, and if this correlation provides a useful indicator, it is likely to be used afterwards. Imagine instead that some of the continually discovered methods of measurement in physics or means of testing in chemistry had not yet been discovered and had therefore not yet been used. They would be unused indicators. The only condition for the existence of unused indicators is the existence of a number of empirical regularities we do not make use of.

(N3) Indicators are more or less reliable. The queen of clubs is a somewhat unreliable sign of an untimely death, and as an indicator of

---

1) In §§ 1 to 3, sign meaning and utterance meaning will not be distinguished.

paranoic tendencies, the reliability of a person's seeing an unusual number of eyes in Rorschach tests is obviously a question of experience. The degree of reliability depends on the form of the empirical correlation; the indicator is more reliable the higher the statistical probability of the thing indicated relative to the indicator. A fingerprint on the trigger of a murder weapon is a very reliable sign for the fact that any person leaving this fingerprint held the weapon in his hand, because it is highly improbable that any two persons should leave the same fingerprints.

(N4) Indicators can generally be regarded as indicating something over a long period of time and can be used in this way without really indicating what they are supposed to indicate, as may possibly be discovered later. For example, a heavy imbalance in trade on the export side was regarded as the decisive sign of a flourishing economy by some mercantilists. If this opinion is no longer held nowadays, the reason is that such enonomies have been discovered to be possibly quite unstable. Divine judgments made manifest by casting lots, trial by fire, water, or duelling were regarded as signs of guilt or innocence up until fairly recent times, not to mention confessions under torture. This means nothing other than that all concerned (or at least almost all) can rely on certain empirical hypotheses for a long period of time and can be wrong in so doing; hopefully, one day the error will be discovered. Such a discovery consists in disproving the empirical hypotheses.

*Conventional signs:*
Arrows point in the direction of the arrowhead.
The game with the well—known thirty—two figures is called 'chess'.
'Bachelor' is synonymous with 'unmarried man'.
A ticker tape parade means a friendly reception.
The whistle of the referee means that the ball is out of play.
A red light means 'Stop!'
Conventional signs have the opposite characteristics of natural indicators:

(C1) Conventional signs have to be used with a given meaning before their meanings can be discovered. In order to use arrows as something pointing in the direction of the arrowhead, one does not have to stumble beforehand — to one's happy surprise — on the fact that they have the felicitous attribute of pointing in the direction of the arrowhead, so that one can make use of this discovery by henceforth pointing with the help of arrows. It is just the other way around; in order that someone should discover that arrows point in the direction of the arrowhead, they would have to have been used with this meaning beforehand.

(C2) If conventional signs are not used they are not signs at all. The word 'chess', as the name for a game, cannot strangely subsist in limbo

6

without being so used. There could be red light signals without their being used as orders to stop; but if they were not used in this way, they would not be orders to stop.

(C3) Conventional signs do not mean what they mean more or less reliably; rather they either mean it or not. Greater or lesser reliability could be attributed to the hypothesis that a sign has this and no other meaning. For instance, in a certain situation in soccer the whistle of the referee does not mean, with more or less probability, that the ball is out of play; the whistle either does or does not mean this. Somebody talking about bachelors in a context excluding universities, knights, buttons, and seals does not with high probability talk about unmarried men; he just talks about unmarried men. What can be more or less reliable is the hypothesis that 'bachelor' has this meaning; but this does not mean that 'bachelor' means what it means with more or less reliability.

(C4) If conventional signs are used with a given meaning, they are *ipso facto* used correctly. If the inhabitants of New York have always celebrated a friendly reception with a ticker tape parade, then it cannot happen that they suddenly (to their horror) realize that this actually is not a friendly greeting, as they have always imagined. It cannot be the case that they try to receive somebody in a friendly manner with a ticker tape parade, but in reality mistakenly express their disdain in so doing. The only thing one could imagine is a small group of recent immigrants mistakenly trying to express their contempt in this way, and in reality giving a friendly reception − contrary to their intention.

Let us hope that the above tests suffice for discarding natural meaning, and head for the next source of confusion.

## § 2 Conventional meaning vs. speaker's meaning

There is a second important distinction to be made between covential meaning and something else. The distinction is that between *meaning y with doing x*, on the one hand, and *saying y with doing x*, on the other. In the first case, the agent means something (with his action); in the second case, he says something (with his action).

In all usual cases, his action is an utterance. Thus we may express the matter in the following way: By uttering x, the speaker means y; or by uttering x, the speaker says y. Instead of 'uttering "It is raining"', we will usually feel free to use 'saying "It is raining"'. However, if we express our pair of contrasts by replacing 'uttering' with 'saying', the second item sounds odd: By saying x, the speaker says y. The oddity is due to a double use of 'say'. It means much the same as 'utter' when prefacing direct speech; not so with indirect speech. This is why there is nothing odd about the following: By saying "It is raining ", the speaker says that it is raining; or: By saying "Es regnet", the speaker says that it is raining.

If 'say' is used in the indirect speech prefacing say, it can be used to answer questions about the meaning of some utterance: "Did the defendant unambiguously promise to marry you?" — "Not exactly, but he said we would live together forever." — "Did he say it in so many words?" — "I do not remember his words, but that is what he said." Used in this way, 'say' can contrast with 'mean' in order to express that what the speaker meant was not what his utterance meant: He said something he did not mean, and he meant something he did not say — for instance, because of a slip of the tongue, or by mixing up names.

Conventional meaning is *conceptually* different from speaker's meaning in the sense that the question, 'What did he mean?' has to be answered by methods different from those appropriate for the question, 'What did he say?'. For whereas the latter question asks what the speaker's utterance meant in his language, information about his language is only empirically relevant for the former (and, of course, very much so). In the present book, we are interested in how it comes about that speakers *say* things; we are not interested in how they manage to *mean* things. In most cases, speakers say what they mean and mean what they say. This is no accident, and it might even be the case that speakers say what they mean because they mean what they say. However, since the concepts are different, this is an open question, and we shall leave it open until we reach ch. V (where I shall argue the opposite).

If what a speaker says is contrasted in this manner with what he means, then from an ontological point of view, what he means appears more down to earth and less suspicious than what he says. For we have a tangible source of what the speaker means — the speaker himself. However, if he can say what he does not mean to say, then how is what he says anchored in innocent reality? The answer: We have to replace the speaker with his language. Just as no utterance is meant save by its speaker, so nothing is said save by virtue of a language. One can mean something with an action outside of language[2] — just trying to get the message over. (At a dinner party, I spill something on my chin without

_____

2) If 'mean' is 'wish to communicate', and if Wittgenstein referred to conventional languages like English or German, then he was wrong in saying: "It is only in a language that I can mean something by something." (*PI* I, p. 18$^e$ fn.) He was right, however, if 'mean' is taken in its usual sense, viz. 'wish to say', or if by 'language' he meant 'human form of life'.

noticing it; my wife looks at me and rubs her chin.) But whenever somebody says something, it is legitimate to ask: "In which language did he
say it?" This is because what he said with his utterance depends on
which language he used.

Replacing the speaker with a language is not, of course, replacing him
with something which is beyond suspicion from an ontological point of
view. (Languages are terribly abstract.) We shall have to show that there
is nothing fishy about this move. At this point, let us simply note that as
an utterance needs a speaker in order to be (subjectively) meant, it needs
a language in order to (objectively) have a meaning. And it is this latter
fact which we are interested in.

## § 3 Conventional meaning and correct understanding

Our path towards an explication of conventional meaning shall be sought
not via a speaker who means something, but via understanding. There is
a close intuitive connection between meaning, as in 'Arrows have the
meaning of pointing in the direction of the arrowhead', and understanding. I shall now try to explicate this connection because it will mark our
intuitive starting point. Let us begin with an innocent translation:

(1) '$z$ means $m$ for $x$' means '$x$ understands $z$ as $m$'.

An example: That arrows, for me, have the meaning of pointing in the
direction of the arrowhead can be put in other words: I understand
arrows as pointing in the direction of the arrowhead. That 'Good morning', for me (non−trivially − remember the author is German), means a
greeting can be expressed by saying that I understand 'Good morning' as
a greeting. Our question will be how to complete (2):

(2) '$z$ means $m$' means ... .

In order to find something with which to fill in the blank let us interpret
some cases either with help of the knowledge that

(A) $z$ means $m$

or else

(B) unaided by such knowledge.

The cases to be considered are (i) − (iv); $m' \neq m$.

(i) $x$ understands $z$ as $m$, whereas $y$ understands $z$ as $m'$.

Interpreting (i) in the darkness of (B), we can only say: $x$ understands $z$
differently from $y$. If we interpret (i) in light of (A), however, we may
say:

(3) $x$ understands $z$ correctly, whereas $y$ understands $z$ incorrectly; in
short: $x$ understands $z$, whereas $y$ doesn't understand $z$.

For example, if I understand arrows as pointing in the direction of the arrowhead, whereas you understand them as pointing in the direction of their tail, we understand them differently. However, since arrows actually have the meaning of pointing in the direction of their heads, I understand them correctly, whereas you understand them incorrectly. I understand them; you don't. (That 'understanding correctly' and 'understanding incorrectly' can be shortened to 'understanding' and 'not understanding' is due, of course, to the fact that, even in its dispositional sense which concerns us here, 'to understand' is an achievement verb.)

(ii) $x$, who understands $z$ as $m$, utters $z$; $y$, who also understands $z$ as $m$, hears $z$.

Interpreting (ii) in case (B), we only infer: $y$ understands $x$. We may also say: $y$ understands what $x$ wants to say with $z$. In light of (A), however, we may say:

(4) $y$ understands $z$.

For instance, if both you and I understand 'Beware of the dog' as a warning, then if I utter it and you hear me, you understand me. However, since 'Beware of the dog' really has this meaning, we may say that you understand my utterance. Compare this with a case where both of us (being German) understand 'Beware of the dog' as meaning 'Look at the dog'; then if I say 'Beware of the dog', you will understand me, but not my utterance (which both of us misunderstand).

(iii) $x$, who understands $z$ as $m$, utters $z$; $y$, who understands $z$ as $m'$, hears $z$.

In case (B), we conclude that $y$ misunderstands $x$, or misunderstands what $x$ wants to say with $z$. However, in light of (A), we may say:

(5) $y$ misunderstands (fails to understand) $z$.

For example, your understanding of 'Come on' is that of a request to get going, whereas my understanding is that of a request to arrive. (I am a *verbum ex verbo* translating German.) Then, if you say 'Come on', I misunderstand you, or misunderstand what you want to say with 'Come on'. However, since 'Come on' actually has the meaning of a request to get going, I misunderstand (fail to understand) not only you, but also your utterance.

Even in case (B), in a certain sense, we might have said that I misunderstood 'Come on'. But then it is crucial that the utterance was yours. For imaginge someone else who, like myself, understands 'Come on' as a request to arrive; if he had uttered 'Come on', I would have understood him, or what he wanted to way with 'Come on'. If I therefore understood 'Come on', what I understood cannot be simply referred to as 'Come on', but only as 'Come on' — as — his — utterance.

(iv)  $x$, who understands $z$ as $m'$, utters $z$; $y$, who understands $z$ as $m$, hears $z$.

As with (iii) in case (B) we will conclude that $y$ misunderstands $x$. In light of (A), however, things are turned around now:

(6)  $x$ misunderstands (fails to understand) $z$.

This is the case where $x$ means to say something, but in fact says something different. For instance, in the course of being introduced to my hostess, I ask her: "How do you do?", because I want to know how she is feeling. But that I meant to ask her does not help me; I have greeted her though I did not mean to do so.

(3)—(6) state facts about (i)—(iv) which obtain only if (A) is the case, i.e. if $z$ means $m$. We can easily explain why this is so if we now complete (2) such as to yield the following translation:

(2)  '$z$ means $m$' means 'understanding $z$ as $m$ is the correct way'. Let $z$ mean $m$. Then (i) because $x$ understands $z$ as $m$, $x$ understands $z$ (correctly), whereas $y$ who understands $z$ differently, understands it incorrectly, or not. (ii) $y$, who understands $z$ as $m$, understands $z$ (correctly). (iii) $y$, who understands $z$ differently, misunderstands (fails to understand) $z$. (iv) $x$, who understands $z$ differently, misunderstands $z$.

Thus if we find a way of informatively interpreting the concept of correct understanding, this will be a step towards a better understanding of the concept of conventional meaning.[3]

§ 4 Correct understanding: The conventional result principle

If instead of asking what correct understanding consists in, we ask how it is manifested, then we find an interesting answer in Wittgenstein's *Philosophical Investigations*. This is not the place for arguing the interpretation in detail.[4] Its gist is as follows: Correctly understanding (in the dispositional sense) the use of a certain expression under given

---

3) It has proved difficult to trace in the literature possible sources where conventional meaning is linked with correct understanding. The first seems to have been R. Doorbar's 'Meaning, Rules, and Behaviour' where the author defends the view that what is essential for meaning is 'appropriate' behavior, which manifests understanding (pp. 34—36, 38f.). B.C. O'Neill, in 'Conventions and Illocutionary Force', p. 226, argued that "the criterion [of the illocutionary act] should be the interpretation the hearers *ought* to adopt, not the interpretation that they do adopt." (Author's italics.) I myself first argued for the identity of the meaning of a sign with the correct way of understanding it in *Die Philosophie der normalen Sprache*, pp. 268—270.
4) See my *Die Philosophie der normalen Sprache*, pp. 56—74.

circumstances essentially involves the disposition to react, as a matter of course, to such a use in the same way as the others do, i.e. the disposition to follow a certain rule in dealing with the expression. What the rule following reactions are like determines in which way the expression, as used under the given circumstances, is understood correctly.

Saying something meaningful is, therefore, a conceptually complex matter. In a given community, from the moment when a certain utterance has been made under certain circumstances, a specific behavioral disposition counts as correct. Responding with this specific behavioral disposition means correctly understanding the utterance in the occurrence sense; having the higher order disposition to respond with the behavioral disposition in question means correctly understanding the utterance in the dispositional sense. Now whoever makes the utterance under the circumstances in question thereby creates a situation in which the specific disposition counts as correct, i.e. a situation where understanding the utterance in that way counts as correct. In other words, he says something with his utterance by way of entitling others to understand him in the way which counts as correct.

Spelled out in detail, this amounts to the conventional result principle: To each an every conventional meaning of an utterance, there corresponds a characteristic bundle of conventional results − rights and duties of speaker, addressee, and possibly third parties, changes in obligations, redistribution of contextual roles and so on. There is nothing systematic about this in Wittgenstein; but there are theoretical approaches in the literature which date back to John L. Austin. In *How to do things with words*[5] he noted that illocutionary acts make it the case that certain subsequent acts are out of order, that they may invite, by convention, certain responses or sequels, that they may commit the speaker to say or not to say certain things. Quite generally, by the illocutionary act the speaker and other participants are committed not to make a $\Gamma 2$ type mistake. Presumably in working out this idea, John R. Searle used such conventional effects as identifying features of an illocutionary act in making them the content of its "essential rule".[6] Essentially the same idea is used in David Lewis' *Convention* by his definition of (so to speak) 'modus−in−use' in terms of the fact that some way of handling utterances is conventional.[7] The idea is that when we look, e.g., for

---

5) Pp. 117, 139; the mistake is described on p. 40 and called "breach" on p. 137.
6) *Speech Acts*, pp. 63, 66f.
7) *Convention*, ch. V.4. With Lewis, there is not always a defining conventional result, but sometimes a defining condition instead; e.g., indicatives are those which

promises in foreign communities, we are looking for utterances that in a specific way commit their speakers to specific future actions.

There are two difficulties with this idea. The first results from the undeniable fact that two utterances with the very same meaning may leave their speakers (or other parites) exposed to different conventionally backed expectations: John Doe's promise to lend Richard Roe one thousand dollars which he needs for a fraudulent money transaction does not commit him in the same way as it does when he needs the money for dental repairs. This difficulty will be met by definitionally linking conventional utterance meanings with conventional results that take effect on pre–existing conventional situations (i.e. situations where parties are exposed to conventionally backed expectations and the like), shifting these situations in specific directions. For instance, rather than obligating him, a request makes its addressee more obligated than he may have already been before. The second difficulty results from the principle's generality. Niceties aside, it states that for any two different conventional utterance meanings, utterances with the first meaning are analytically tied to a conventional result different from that of utterances with the second meaning. One may doubt whether this could possibly be shown to hold generally. However, the proof of the pudding is in the eating, and the most successful counter to the second difficulty consists in actually working out convincing conventional results for plenty of utterance meanings.[8] As far as this proves to be successful, utterances with given meanings could then be discovered via their conventional results, rather than via speakers' intentions.

## § 5 Conventional systems evolving into languages

To native Anglo–Saxon speakers, the very idea of even momentarily forgetting about the speaker while pondering upon the meaning of his utterance looks like abstracting from essential facts. It is all too natural to feel that what a speaker means by his utterance is extremely important

----

Continued:

speakers conventionally *try to utter only in case they are true*. (178f.) However, if such an indicative is uttered, it will rouse conventionally backed expectations which correspond precisely to that condition. For instance, if the utterance turns out to be false, it will be claimed that the speaker has an excuse. – The first explicit statement of the conventional result principle seems to be due to I. Heim, *Zum Verhältnis von Wahrheitsbedingungen – Semantik und Sprechakttheorie*, pp. 12f.; for a recent application, see R. Brandom's 'Asserting'.

8) Complete lists of the findings which are used in the present study can be found in Appendix I and II.

for what his utterance means — that utterance meaning is utterer's meaning. This feeling is at home in the idea that language not only *is* a means of communication, but also must be *explained* and *understood* as a tool for people who mean to get their messages over. In its most vivid form, the principle that without speakers' intentions there would be no meanings can be illustrated with reference to language evolution : The first instance of non—conventional communicative behavior is one where somebody has intentions which are complex enough to earn him the description of meaning something by what he does.[9] Behaving in such ways is learned and passed on from generation to generation because it is successful;[10] as soon as enough people master such ways, they come to be conventionally expected. Utterances have acquired their conventional meanings because speakers have come to commit themselves conventionally to mean what they are expected to mean.

Let me illustrate the present approach with a somewhat different fairy tale: Here we begin with a pre—linguistic group with rich conventional behavior; i.e., there are many kinds of actions which, if performed in specific circumstances, expose their agents to certain expectations on part of the other group members. They also have conventional effects on other parties to the situation. Because of their group survival value, some such actions specialize in conventional results: performing them retains no interesting result over an above the conventional one. Insofar as the conventional result can be described as that of an utterance with a given meaning, performing the action becomes making an utterance with this meaning. Therefore, saying something by performing such actions now belongs to the behavioral repertoire available to the group members. They learn to handle this repertoire, e.g. to bring about only conventional results whose burden they can bear and to take advantage of conventional results produced by others. Eventually they learn that, of the results of what they do, others will take advantage, and having learned this, they use their competence intentionally. E.g., S does something which conventionally permits someone A to rely, at the expense of S, on the fact that p (i.e., S informs A that p); S will usually do this only when he can bear the costs, i.e. if p is true; therefore, A will generally believe that p is true. From the time when S has become accustomed to this effect of such an utterance, he can intend to convince A of the truth of p by making the utterance.

---

9) J. Bennett, 'The Meaning—Nominalist Strategy', pp. 146—149; *Linguistic Behaviour*, pp. 138—141.
10) St. Schiffer, *Meaning*, pp. 120 — 128.

Both illustrative pictures will of course agree on language persever-ance: lest conventional language were used for intentional communication, it would simply vanish along with the civilizational level sustained by it. But whereas intentional use creates the tool, so to speak, in the "meaning is where something is meant" idea, according to the present approach, intentional communication makes use of a tool which developed prior to its intentional use.

## § 6 Communication: Redistributing situational roles

To these historical fairy tales correspond different pictures of what is at the heart of communication. The 'meaning is where something is meant' theory views communication as a combined effort, by the speaker to disclose his intentions, and by the hearer to grasp them. The conven-tionalist theory, on the other hand, views ongoing communication as an ongoing redistribution of situational roles. In offering to put him up, the speaker makes himself liable to give the addressee a bed if the offer is accepted, and binds the addressee to either accept or decline. In reporting that the bridge is destroyed, the speaker authorizes the addressee to act on this fact, accepting liability for damages which the addressee suffers because of an unnecessary detour. In requesting to help him in carrying the ladder to the apple — tree, the speaker confers upon the addressee an increase in obligation to help him (the details of this increase depending on further facts about their social rules in general).

By way of redistributing situational roles, further effects can be achieved, be the achievement intended or not. Let me illustrate this by a look at bridge. By bidding or passing, I modify my own rights (using up my right for this round) and the rights and duties of the next player ( he has now to overbid or to pass); by playing a card, I offer the trick to the party with the highest card or trump. These are fundamental facts about bidding and playing. However, I can achieve further ends, and these may become so prominent that they appear to be even crucial for an under-standing of what I do.

E.g., in bidding one of hearts as the dealer, I confer upon my partner the position to act on the fact that I hold a biddable suit of hearts. Usual-ly, he will act on this fact, while even believing it to be a fact; this is something I have achieved. After some practice, the achievement will normally be an indended one. This my partner will come to learn; and after I have learned that he did this, I can bid one of hearts with the intention that he recognize my intention that he believe me to hold a biddable suit of hearts.

Or if, as the first to play, I play my lowest card of clubs (clubs have not been bidden), I thereby obligate my partner to play his highest card of clubs (disregarding some niceties, and invoking the general competitive game rule of trying to win). He will usually do this, thus either winning the trick or forcing the single player to spend one of his high honours. With the increased probability that I now hold the highest card of clubs, the rule of trying to win obligates him to lead clubs as soon as seems appropriate; and other things being equal, he will do this. In a parallel process as above, I can come to play my lowest card of a non − bidden suit with the intention that he recognize my intention that he lead this suit as soon as possible.

Because the opening bid is almost never the final one, and because if I open the play with a move like the one just described it would normally not matter much if I did something else instead, the underlying conventional effects remain pretty uninteresting, whereas the parasitic effects become prominent. The 'speaker' bids as he does because he wants to convince his partner about some feature of his hand, and he leads the suit he does because he wants his partner to do some other thing; his partner, the 'addressee', will grasp just these points which are what is salient for both of them about their communication. Nonetheless, the redistribution of situational roles is at the heart of the matter.

This all sounds a bit odd, and one may well wonder how, for instance, an author redistributes situational roles by publishing a book in philosophy of language? But he is sure to do just that − let one single item in his book be different, and he will be exposed to different arguments which others may launch against him by virtue of the fact that he 'uttered' the text as a contribution to a discussion.

## § 7 The strategy of language description

I shall attempt to spell out the intuition which was sketched in the foregoing sections in a way which has become a standard method in philosophy of language, viz. in describing what a theory has to look like which covers whatever can be said in some natural language. However, only the trunk of such a theory will be described; the part about items which interest philosophers of language most will be left out, viz. the part which tells us how the meanings of sub − sentential expressions contribute to things like sentence meaning, reference, predication, etc. Syntax will also go unmentioned. Therefore, with a few possible exceptions, there will be no contribution to clarifying any interesting semantical notion.

This disappointing mutilation results from a certain methodological strategy, viz. from describing the intended model ostensively. Instead of generally defining a framework for describing languages, I shall demonstrate how it works if applied to a concrete case study. Because this is a cumbersome procedure, some space will have to be spent, in § 17, on justifying it; here it may suffice to point to one consequence: The case under scrutiny will have to be the whole of some natural language, including the system of social conventions which it is embedded in. For my demonstrative purpose, the comprehensiveness requirement is more important than a desire to say something about interesting semantical notions; unfortunately, the requirement excludes, as demonstration models, languages with syntax and sub−sentential expressions, simply because they are too rich to be studied as wholes. What remains, then, are three main topics:

(1)  What are sentence meanings, and how is a theory to be tested which ascribes sentence meanings to expressions? The answer will be: The theory must be unequalled in yielding correct predictions on utterance meanings.

(2)  What are utterance meanings, and how is a theory to be tested which ascribes utterance meanings to uses of expressions under certain circumstances? The answer will be: The theory must be unequalled in yielding correct predictions on certain changes in conventional situations.

(3)  How are these changes in conventional situations to be analyzed, and how is the description of a situation as a relevant conventional situation to be tested? As an answer, the relevant vocabulary will be analyzed in terms of empirically testable facts about social rule following behavior, the analysis being free from concepts whose use would render the enterprise uninformative.

I shall work my way from the hard empirical conventional facts to be dealt with in (3) through the theoretical level of utterance meanings in (2) up to sentence meanings in (1), the highest theoretical level which I shall reach. (In § 39, it will be explained why this is the level of sentence meaning although the corresponding expressions have no structure.) Thus the first task is to analyze the relevant conventional facts in terms of rule−following behavior.

# Chapter II
# Compliance with rules

## § 8 The weak Hart analysis of rule – guided behavior

If a group uses a conventional language, then some behavioral patterns are required among its members. A behavioral pattern consists in performing a given kind of behavior $B$ if involved in a certain situation $S$; if it is required, then exhibiting $B$ in $S$ is required. Disregarding a point which I shall discuss in § 9, the core of Hart's analysis is as follows:[11]

In a group, behavior $B$ is required in situation $S$
translates into:

(1)  Members of the group seldom openly depart from $B$ in $S$ ;
(2)  if they deviate, they are subject to sanctions on the part of the other members of the group;
(3)  these sanctions are generally accepted.

Condition (1) requires that $B$ is usual in $S$; its function is to distinguish the empirical validity of what we might call 'implicit rules' − in this case the empirical validity of the rule that $B$ ought to be exhibited in $S$ − from that of rules which are only acknowledged as valid by members of the group without being generally complied with, however.[12] In developed societies, the most prominent examples of such rules are some legal norms whose binding force is not questioned; however, people quite generally get around them. Such rules are not my subject matter; they will further diverge from implicit rules with regard to condition (2) since they require some particular authority.

Furthermore, condition (1) excludes the following case from our analysis: Members of the group very often fail to exhibit $B$ in $S$, even when it is noticeable to other members; they suffer the formal or informal punishments which ensue without resistance; and their tendency to conform even increases after the punishment. However, after a very short time, they fall back to their old habits. $B$ would seem to be, not something which members of the group require from each other, but an

---

11) H.L.A. Hart, *The Concept of Law*, pp. 54−56.
12) In her paper 'Agreement, Conventions, and Language', M. Gilbert has argued (against D. Lewis) that conventions of the 'first time when $x$ happens' type (which are all due to explicit agreement ) may, by their very formulation, extend to exactly one situation only (see esp. sect. 4 and 5). This would not even violate the spirit of the first condition (let alone its letter). For the agent's disposition is still one of reacting to a *type* of situation: a situation of type $F$ such that no other of the same type has preceded it.

ideal to which they try to push each other. A class of such behavioral patterns would resemble a life free from sin. The good Roman Catholic often falls into sin, says the prayer which his father confessor enjoins on him as a penance, makes firm resolutions to turn away from sin — and when temptation comes, he gives right in. A group of good Roman Catholics is not my central paradigm of a group in which God's commandments and those of his Holy Church count as the correct ways of behavior. The analysis is not to capture a group's ideology.

Condition (2) states a dispositional property. Its vagueness is on its surface; I shall not comment on this vagueness because I take it to be fruitful. On the one hand, leaving the condition vague allows us to speak of degrees to which $B$ is required in $S$; and I think we ought to be able to speak of such degrees. On the other hand, I cannot hope to give a general account of the facts, social and other, upon which the actual execution of impending sanctions depends.

However, owing to my strictly non—intentionalist approach to meaning, I am bound to comment on a question about condition (2). The question is how a sanction manages to be directed against a given deviation, and consequently, which facts are relevant for it to be directed against a deviation from $B$, rather than against a deviation from $B'$, if the behavior which the sanction follows upon deviates both from $B$ and from $B'$. For example: I crowd into the line in front of the movie box office. In doing this, I deviate from the rule never to crowd into line, and sanctions will follow immediately — people will simply push me out of the line, or something like this. However, their very reaction might also constitute a sanction against my deviation from the following putative rules: Never to enter lines, not to buy movie tickets, not to enter lines from the left, not to wear dinner jackets in cinema lobbies (I happen to be wearing one), not to approach whites as a latino (I happen to be a Puertorican), and so on. Under which circumstances is their pushing me out of the line a sanction against the deviation from one rule rather than a sanction against a deviation from some other rules?[13]

I have an easy answer because I have no qualms in bringing all philosophical guns to bear on a problem as long as the guns are not particularly suspicious in the context in question. I invoke counterfactual conditionals. Pushing me out of the line is a sanction against my crowding into line, because I would have been exposed to it whenever I crowded into a line; it is not a sanction against any of the deviations from the other

---

13) We must not say, of course: "But no such rules are valid!" Which rules are valid depends upon deviations from which ones are exposed to sanctions.

putative rules if it is not the case that among these rules there is one such that whenever I were to deviate from this rule, I would have been exposed to being pushed out of the line.

I cannot contribute to a clarification of the concept of a sanction. Why is pushing someone out of line something which members of the group treat as negative, instead of treating it like a friendly slap on someone's back? Hart is able to pass over this problem because his problem is different from mine — he presupposes his group to have a language comprising things which are recognizable as 'criticisms'. Explaining what it means for something to count as unwelcome in a group whose language — if any — is not understood is a problem of a different order of magnitude. Above all, the explanation would require us to state behavioral criteria for what members of the group like and dislike.

The function of condition (2), of course, is to distinguish simple general habits from rules which are implicitly complied with. Watching one of the evening newscasts on TV seems to be a general habit in West Germany. However, there seems to be no pressure to do so. Condition (2) would be empirically idle (though not conceptually unnecessary), if everything most people do would be socially enforced. However, it is not empirically idle — let alone conceptually unimportant.

Condition (3) mainly serves to draw a line — or better, to establish a no‑man's‑land between controversial and non‑controversial rules (i.e. between rules which fight for obedience and rules which go without saying). In order to count as correct in $S$, $B$ must be non‑controversial; this is why condition (3) states that instead of resisting, trespassers must accept sanctions. I do not enrich 'accepting' beyond failing to resist, or giving in. The minimum enrichment would consist in the requirement that if someone accepts a sanction, his propensity to conform to the rule is strengthened. I prefer a relatively poor interpretation of condition (3), because I want to keep the concept of a situation in which behavioral patterns are required as purely descriptive as possible. The minimum enrichment would entail that behavioral patterns which count as correct, at least in part, count so because they are socially enforced.

Note that our conditions do not require anything linguistic in connection with correctness; there need not be any normative tradition, oral or written. Note also that no group member needs to know which rules he follows. All that follows from conditions (1) − (3) is that group members know that certain behavioral patterns are correct *insofar as* such knowledge is manifested by fulfilling conditions (1) − (3). If intended to be one, Warnock's[14] argument to the contrary is obviously guided, and, I think, mislead, by a conception which is restricted to enacted rules.

## § 9 Why dismiss the 'internal aspect'?

Hart's literal conditions for the existence of rules are as follows:[15]
    (a)  There must be general conformance to the pattern of behavior in question;
    (b)  deviations incur criticism and pressure;
    (c)  deviations are accepted as reasons for criticism of the deviations;
    (d)  the members of the group must look upon the rule from an "internal point of view".

(a) corresponds to (1), (b) to (2). (3) is a generalized version of (c). Hart is undoubtedly right that some such condition is necessary; for it helps to distinguish between rules that are deeply entrenched and others that are in dispute. But I fear that in our context, this condition either is too narrow − if it is intended to demand that the sanctions and the forms of accepting them be verbal − or its range of application is too narrow if, where sanctions are non − verbal, it simply does not apply. This is why I replaced criticisms with sanctions and the acceptance of a certain way of justifying criticisms with the acceptance of sanctions.

I did not accept condition (d), or any equivalent. This is why my concept is weaker than Hart's concept. Hart distinguishes two kinds of people, all conforming to conditions (a) − (c) (or (1) − (3), for that matter). The first kind of people do not really accept the rule; they do not regard themselves as being bound to follow it. If they deviate, they do so with a god conscience, so to speak. If they comply with the rule in a case where they would prefer to deviate, they comply for reasons of prudence. For instance, they are afraid of sanctions. Their way of regarding the rule is what Hart terms the "external point of view". (It is a group member's point of view and must not be confused with the observer's point of view.) Hart contrasts these people with what, in his view, must constitute the vast majority, people who accept the rule from the bottom of their heart. For them, compliance is taken for granted. They deviate remorsefully and would be ashamed if caught deviating.

There is a big difference between rules which exist in groups whose members largely share the internal or external points of view. But I think that the difference is much bigger between groups whose members largely share the external point of view vis à vis their rules, and groups where

---

14) G.J. Warnock, *The Object of Morality*, p. 48f.
15) *L.c.*, pp. 54−56, 86−88, 96, 99−101.

there exist no rules at all. This view leads me to the opinion that the internal aspect is superfluous in the present context for two reasons.

The first reason ist this: It seems to be impossible to distinguish people who comply with a rule from an internal or from an external point of view without prior understanding of their linguistic behavior. At any rate, I have not been able to devise criteria which do not rely on such knowledge. This is confirmed by the literature; all criteria which are given there refer exclusively to the different things which 'external' and 'internal' people are prone to say.[16]

The second reason is more important, however: I fail to see a point in this distinction. The two types of rule — following behavior should not be distinguished because purely 'external' compliance is, or may be bound to be unstable.[17] For if we accept such empirical hypotheses in order to dismiss certain conceivable kinds of social behavior as uninteresting (because unlikely to exist), we ought to accept other wellfounded empirical hypotheses as well, especially the following one: Either there are so few 'externals' in the group that they are covered by our generality clauses, or there are sufficiently many so that even condition (2) no longer holds. (For reasons of prudence someone may get along with a rule in trying to avoid sanctions and in not resisting sanctions; but prudence would then demand that he does not punish others for deviations.) Empirically, 'externalist' groups are likely not to fit the definition; thus we do not need a special condition to exclude them for empirical reasons.

Neither should the external point of view be interpreted as one which regards social norms as directions for use in successful social behavior. This may have been Hart's motive for introducing the condition, and it has been brought out very clearly by Morris[18] (whom I join in rejecting the 'internal point of view' requirement). There is, of course, a difference between 'rules' which we follow in order to grow large potatoes or to avoid burning our hands, and social rules. However, this does not mean that there might not be social rules which we follow for the sole reason of avoiding punishment from any fellow group member whatsoever. I think the difference is sufficiently explained by the difference

---

16) This includes Hart himself (*l.c.* e.g. pp. 56, 99), as well as G.P. Baker, 'Defeasability and Meaning'; P.M.S. Hacker, 'Hart's Philosophy of Law'; Herbert Morris, 'Hart's Concept of Law',p. 1459. Hacker's description (p.16) of the external point of view would nicely suit the internal point of view, if linguistic behavior were left out.

17) "Unhealthy", in the words of William L. McBride, in 'The Acceptance of a Legal System', p. 394.

18) *L.c.*, p. 1460.

between experiencing boiling water on one's hand and eperiencing hostility on the part of the group in which one wants to feel at home.

Imagine us to have found, along the outline sketched in chapters III and VI, a plausible description of our group's hypothetical language. Up until then, we would not have made use of any understanding of their linguistic behavior. Now we turn back to investigating their attitudes towards their own social rules. Probably their verbal behavior will reflect the internal point of view. If, however, we find out — to our surprise — that a great number of group members share the external point of view, we shall have to inquire why, in spite of this fact, the overall symmetry with regard to conditions (1), (2), and (3) can hold all the same. But we shall not have reason to rewrite the rules which we take them to comply with.

§ 10 Hart attacks repelled

Hart's analysis of the existence of rules has met with criticism.[19] One point of minor importance: Raz has argued[20] that a general practice which is universally considered as reasonable and which in addition is sanctioned does not thereby suffice for the existence, in this group, of the rule to follow the practice. I have not found a convincing argument, either in Raz or elsewhere, why compliance with rules might not sometimes have a point which is obvious to the whole community.

Further criticisms all seem to spring from confusions which are worthwhile to uncover. E.g., Hacker[21] has argued that if we follow Hart, we are analytically precluded from attempts at explicit moral reform:

> "A moralist frequently declares an act to be morally obligatory, and will not withdraw his claim upon being told that its omission is not viewed by most members of his social group in the critical reflective way which, on Hart's account, is analytically involved in the notion of obligation...Hart...provides a social—fact analysis of 'duty' in terms of reactive attitudes, critical responses, demands for certain patterns of conduct, and the like. Hence, in the absence of these social facts it must be illegitimate for a moral reformer or critic to declare an act to be a duty in the primary sense of the term 'moral duty'." (p. 168)

This is grotesque and springs from lumping together, on p. 161, three

---

19) I am indebted to Professor Hart for information on critical literature.
20) J. Raz, *Practical Reason and Norms*, pp. 55f.
21) P.M.S. Hacker, 'Sanction Theories of Duty'.

conditions which, according to Hart, identify duty — imposing *rules*, and five conditions which, according to Hart, identify a *social situation in which such a rule exists* in a given group. In thus identifying 'x is a duty — imposing rule' with 'x is such and such and exists in a given group', Hacker can, of course, easily show that nothing is a rule unless it is already generally complied with. We are therefore well — advised to distinguish the question, 'Is x a rule?' from the question, 'Does x exist in a given group?' (Or 'Is x complied with in a given group?')

The same confusion has led Raz[22] to state, as an argument against Hart's analysis: "Rules need not be practiced in order to be rules." Of course not; Hart never said so. From the imputed identification, it is clear that Raz can conclude that "the practice theory...deprives rules of their normative character." (p. 56) Small wonder; all that Hart's 'practice theory' does is to deprive the empirical existence of rules of any normative character. Exactly the same confusion occurs with Singer:[23]

> "How can a *rule* be a *practice*?...For this seems to me to imply that it is not a rule at all, in any accepted sense. Can such a 'rule' (practice) be broken? violated? formulated? Can it be said to require, prohibit, or permit anything?" (p. 213; author's italics.)

Dworkin[24] has made a similar point against what he labels the 'social rule theory' (referring to Hart's position):

> "the social rule theory...believes that the social practice *constitutes* a rule which the normative judgement accepts ..." (1972, p. 867; 1977, p. 57; author's italics.)

Talk of 'constituting' (also on p. 860 = 51) is simply a bit less clear than Hacker's and Raz' wording of the confusion. However, Dworkin adds an interesting connection between the existence of duty — imposing rules and the existence of duties:

> "Under what circumstances do duties and obligations arise? Hart's answer may be summarized in this way. Duties exist when social rules exist providing for such duties. Such social rules exist when the practice — conditions for such rules are met. These practice — conditions are met when the members of a community behave in a certain way; this behavior *constitutes* a social rule, and imposes a duty." (p. 858f. = 49; author's italics.)

---

22) *L.c.*, p. 53.
23) G. Singer, 'Hart's Concept of Law'.
24) M. Dworkin, 'Social Rules and Legal Theory', also as ch. III of the same author's *Taking Rights Seriously*.

"The existence of the social rule, and therefore the existence of the duty, is simply a matter of fact." (p. 859 = 50)

That a duty exists (or to put it more modestly: that there is a duty), would normally be taken to be a normative fact; thus what Dworkin believes to have found in Hart seems to be terribly wrong. Let us note, however, that in the first quotation, "Duties exist" cannot render Hart's position unless it is expanded to "Duties exist relative to a group's social rules"; but then the argument collapses. It is designed to show that Hart confuses two roles:

"When a sociologist says that a particular community 'has' or 'follows' a particular rule, like the no−hat−in−church rule, he means only to describe the behavior of that community in a certain respect. He means only to say that members of that community suppose that they have a particular duty, and not that he agrees. But when a member of the community himself appeals to a rule, for the purpose of criticizing his own or someone else's behavior, then he does not simply mean to describe the behavior of other people, but to evaluate it. He means not simply that others believe that they have a certain duty, but that they *do* have that duty." (p. 859 = 50; author's italics.)

Hart is, of course, busy to explain the sociologist's empirical assertion of the group's compliance with the rule, not the group member's normative assertion of this same rule's validity. Unfortunately, Dworkin now conjures up two different rules:

"The sociologist, we might say, is asserting a *social* rule, but the churchgoer is asserting a *normative* rule...Hart...denies, at least as to the case he discusses, that these two sorts of assertions can be said to assert two different sorts of rules." (p. 860 = 5of.; author's italics.)

Asserting, as a social fact, the existence of a rule is not, of course, asserting a social rule; nor is the rule normative by virtue of being normatively asserted. Now because, in Dworkin's view, Hart identifies *the existence of the rule*, i.e. Dworkin's "*social* rule", with Dworkin's "*normative* rule", i.e. the normative assertion of the rule by group members, he surprisingly imputes to Hart the idea that anyone who normatively asserts a rule *ipso facto* empirically asserts that it is complied with in his group − which is of course wrong (pp. 861 − 867 = 51 − 58).

What, then, are we to learn from this criticism? My proposal: Let us carefully distinguish the rule "Do *B* in *S*" both from the statement "The rule 'Do *B* in *S*' exists in this group" and from the normative assertion (made by some member of the group) "The rule that one has to do $B$ in $S$ is a valid rule". That is all there is to these arguments.

## § 11 An attractive alternative: Lewis conventions

To the best of my knowledge, use of Hart's 1961 analysis of the existence of rules has, in the philosophy of language, remained an almost exclusive delight of the present author ever since the above ideas were first sketched out in 1974.[25] Two reasons might account for this neglect (the analysis was not unknown to philosophers of language; see the references to Baker and Hacker in §§ 9 and 10).

On the one hand, the very question 'What is a rule for using language?' strongly suggests that rules for the use of language prescribe or prohibit typical linguistic actions, like applying words to things, or like being sincere in making utterances. Rules whose group validity constitutes use of a language, by this group, seem to be characterized by governing a small section of human behavior. The idea that rules should provide a short cut from meanings of linguistic utterances and expressions to regulated behavior — something like 'If $p$ means $Q$ then $p$ ought to be sincerely uttered only of it is the case that $Q$' — is intimately related to this suggestion. Hart's analysis does not hint at such matters, of course.

On the other hand, David Lewis proposed a very attractive analysis of convention in 1969.[26] This analysis has two advantages: it provides a general concept of convention which may apply to any conventional behavior whatsoever; and, under the label of 'conventions of truthfulness', an application to linguistic behavior, such that linguistic conventions state what members of a linguistic community are expected to do if, in the language they use, uttering signs in given situations has given meanings; e.g. to try to utter a sign uttering which has, in the given situation, the meaning of a report that $p$, only when it is the case that $p$. Lewis' analysis thus fulfills the expectations noted above — linguistic

---

25) *Die Philosophie der normalen Sprache*, ch. 7; see also G. Grewendorf, 'Explizit performative Äußerungen und Feststellungen', pp. 203−213.

26) *Convention*, ch. 1. For a particularly perspicuous exposition, see Kemmerling's Munich Ph.D. Dissertation, *Konvention und sprachliche Kommunikation*. This small monograph contains much substantial criticism, as well as an improvement which saves what Kemmerling takes to be Lewis' central ideas. Further critical discussions will be mentioned below; I disclaim the critique raised in 'Listener−Oriented Versus Speaker−Oriented Analysis of Conventional Meaning', pp. 73f. — Many of my considerations in §§ 11 to 15 bear equally on the partly parallel analysis found in Stephen Schiffer's book *Meaning*. A mishap of this important work was that it suffered under a time−lag in publication.

conventions which regulate a section of typical linguistic behavior and which provide a short cut from meaning to behavior. But by being embedded in an analysis of convention in general, this analysis leaves out any tinge of adhocness.

As I shall make clear in later sections (see esp. §§ 16, 23, 27, 44), I don't expect those rules whose group validity constitutes use of a language, by this group, to regulate a typical section of behavior, or to provide a short cut from meaning to behavior. I will not present an equivalent to Lewis' 'conventions of truthfulness', and weak Hart rules will not play their roles. Lewis' conventions in general, however, could well take over the roles which weak Hart rules will come to play. I think it is better if they don't, and I shall defend this view in §§ 12 to 14. My argument will concern what I take to be the bakground ideas of Lewis' analysis; therefore, I shall sketch out his analysis in light of its presumed background ideas. Consider the following stories: (*Ceteris paribus* requirements, notorious from rational decision theory, are stated once only, and in brackets.)

(1)   One agent,[27] one solution: (Above all) Mother wants to enjoy Child's company once a day. Her problem is how to achieve this. If she knows she can (best) entice Child by offering a hot meal at 7 p.m. (Child grows hungry at 7 p.m. and comes to the dinner table when hungry), then it is rational for her to offer a meal at 7. Therefore, if she is rational, she will offer a hot meal at 7.

(2)   Two agents, one solution: Mother wants to enjoy Child's company, Child wants a good meal. Mother knows she can enjoy Child's company by serving a good meal when Child shows up; Child knows he can get food by showing up when Mother serves dinner. Both know that dinner takes about thirty minutes, that Mother cannot be finished before 7 and that Child watches T.V. at 7.30 p.m. Mother and Child know everything stated so far. If each takes the other for rational and if each knows they do this, then it is rational for Mother to serve dinner at 7 and for Child to show up; for it is then rational for them to rely on each other's doing what is required, in which case doing their own part is as rational as is Mother's serving dinner in (1).

(3)   One agent, two best solutions: Mother persists with her love — for — food idea; however, Child can be won over by food all day. Since Mother does not care whether dinner is at 7 or 8, she has the additional 'problem' of choosing the time. This she can solve by flipping a coin.

---

27)   Child is an agent, too; but his problem is not considered.

(4)   Two agents, two best solutions: Same story as in (2); however, 8 o'clock is also available for both. Mother and Child now face an additional problem. As in (3), and unlike (2), there is more than one solution, i.e. more than one optimal combination of serving dinner at 7 or 8 and showing up at 7 or 8; but unlike (2), neither Mother nor Child can independently choose what to do. Lewis calls this kind of situation a 'coordination problem'. This may − and in our case will − be a 'recurrent coordination problem'; as long as Mother longs for Child's company and Child seeks food at home, it will recur every day. In principle, the problem can be solved anew each day, e.g. by Mother leaving a note when she leaves in the morning. In many cases, however, a different solution will emerge. By whatever process, Child comes to expect that Mother will set the table at 7, and Mother comes to expect that Child will show up at 7. Every evening at 7, Child shows up because of his expectation and Mother sets the table because of hers. The recurrent coordination problem is thus solved by "a regularity in behavior produced by a system of expectations".[28] If we apply Lewis' definition to our case, we get:

Serving dinner at 7, on Mother's part, and showing up at 7, on Child's part, is a convention between Mother and Child because:

(Kernel) They behave in this way; they expect each other to behave such; both prefer simultaneity of dinner serving and showing up to non − simultaneity; each would opt for 8 o'clock on condition that the other does.

(Common knowledge of kernel) Both have noticed that they have kept this regularity in the past; because both noticed that they have, they may safely assume each other to have noticed that they did; and because they did, they may safely assume
− that they are disposed to behave in this way,
− that they expect each other to behave such,
− that they prefer simultaneity to chaos,
− and that each would opt for 8, if the other did.[29]

Why common knowledge of the kernel? It makes operative expectations

---

28) *Convention*, p. 118.
29) For Lewis' definition see *Convention*, p. 78, in combination with the definition of 'common knowledge', p. 56, and of 'indicating', p. 52f. I presuppose that past conformity is the 'basis' for common knowledge of conventions referred to in the definition of common knowledge. Because the example is a two − alternative two − persons problem, the application is simpler than the general definition. The modification in 'Languages and Language', p. 5, is of no concern in the present context.

rational.[30] It is not only rational for Child to show up at 7 o'clock because he expects Mother to serve dinner; it is also rational for him to expect this because, by virtue of his share of common knowledge, he may safely assume that she has rational expectations and preferences which will lead her to serve dinner.

The leading ideas in this analysis are: (1) Conventional behavior is a kind of collective problem — solving. If no convention is followed, everyone is likely to be worse off; conventions are followed because people want to make sure that they are doing as well as possible. (2) Conventions are solutions about which it would make sense to 'convene' even for rational people who always choose the best solution; for there is more than one best solution, and which one should be choosen depends on the choices of others. In this sense, conventions are arbitrary. (3) In a vague sense of 'know', people can or do know their conventions in a way which bolsters the impression of conventions as cleverly applied tools.

Lewis' concept of a convention is, of course, much richer than Hart's concept of existing rules. This is precisely my reason for using the latter. In §§ 12 to 14 I shall argue that Lewis' concept is so rich that, among the groups of humans we are interested in, there are no Lewis conventions, and that if there were, we could never find this out. I shall further argue that not all behavioral patterns which are relevant for determining which language a group is using, and are such by virtue of being socially sanctioned, are conventional in Lewis' sense. Whether or not readers can accept this latter argument depends, of course, on how convincing my overall approach to linguistic meaning will look to them; there will be no disagreement that the regularities to be referred to in this context are, in fact, no Lewis conventions.[31] Thus Lewis conventions will be put to test for a job which they were not designed to do in *Convention*. If I am right, then there are no living 'conventions of truthfulness' either; but showing this is a by — product, not an aim of my argument.

---

30) In 'Languages and Language', p. 6, Lewis states a different motive: Common knowledge of the kernel is to ensure its stability. I think that such an empirical claim can be convincing only if rationality is taken to be widespread and effective to a high degree; and it is this assumption which strikes the eye when Lewis hopes to ensure the stability of a convention by other means than, say, lack of flexibility.

31) In some papers which are critical of Lewis, there are various arguments which are intended to show that Lewis' concept is not our established concept of convention. (See Burge, 'On Knowledge and Convention'; Jamieson, 'David Lewis on Convention'; Gilbert, 'Agreements, Conventions, and Language'.) This is not a point I wish to make; however, the examples given there furnish further evidence for the latter — and more trivial — of my points, viz. that Lewis conventions, if they existed, would make up only a tiny fragment of linguistically relevant behavior.

## § 12 No rigid problem – solving

For conventional behavior to be collective problem – solving of the type illustrated in § 11, parties to a convention should be sufficiently *rational* to do what, according to their actual *expectations*, will bring about what they *prefer* most.[32] If in our above story, Child is feeble – minded (in the clinical sense) but regularly shows up at the table when he smells dinner, we would say that he reacts to the smell rather than that he pays attention to what is necessary for satisfying his hunger. If Mother is unaware of the probability of Child's showing up, it would be inappropriate to say that she set the table because she expected him to come, even if she could have known it. If, unknown to both Mother and Child, it is useful for them to meet once a day, we would not say that, for this reason, meeting satisfies one of their preferences.

Lewis starts from a picture of man acting rationally, a picture which he takes for granted. However, people might grant the contrary, and I think it is an open question which side the burden of proof lies with. Man may be viewed according to a general character which I hope to call to mind by recalling only some of its traits. One such trait is that in reflective behavior there is a wide – spread reluctance to even consider unwelcome side – effects, if the main object is attractive; another an almost universal lack of consistency, e.g. where the methodical search for a leak or for a short – circuit is spoiled by spontaneously following up sparks of genius which prove useless. A third and perhaps contrary one is sticking to one's premeditated course regardless of how the situation is developing, frequent not only with single individuals but also with decision processes involving several people where prior decisions often count as sacrosanct. A fourth feature may be illustrated by one of Lewis' examples of conventional behavior.[33] If people are out in the forest to gather something – wood, mushrooms, blueberries –, what you observe is a strong tendency for them to flock together and to work over the same places and bushes; exactly the same thing happens when the dinner table is cleared – as soon as someone begins to gather up plates,

---

32) Because Lewis is concerned with coordination problems, parties to the convention must also know what their commonly accepted alternatives are; this point as well as two further ones, viz. that they know *why* just these are their alternatives (i.e. that they know each others' preferences) and that they *reasonably* expect each other to do certain things (i.e. that they have evidence warranting their expectations) will be discussed in § 14.

33) *Convention*, p. 45. I do not wish to deny that a more economical division of labor would develop if Princeton staff were camping.

someone else invariably will follow suit. (Recall how people cease to care for what they do, or worse, for what is done to them, if they are many.) — This list is quite unsystematic; its sole function is to get hold of a general character of human behavior (much as we may cite single features of a person's behavior in order to remind someone of this person's character) — a character which I take to be manifest from everyday experience, even if it does not figure prominently in rational decision theory.

Perhaps it is also useful to remember from the start that problem solving differs from problem avoiding. Take, for instance, a colony of ants which, one sunny summer, has settled beneath a large rock. Remove the rock and you will find that the ants, in what might anthropomorphically be described as a cooperative, disciplined, patriotic endeavor, rescue their eggs from the dangerous exposure, reassembling in less than an hour to a safer place. However, if we assume — as perhaps we should — that their behavior is purely instinctive in contrast to intelligent, we would not say that they solved their problem collectively; rather we would say that each individual's repertoire of instinctive behavior is such that in this situation the outcome of all is favorable for the colony's and thereby, for each individual's continued existence. Of course, if they judged the situation as we would judge it in their place, if they loved life as we love life, and if they were as prudent as we sometimes are (though typically not in such panic situations), then we could say in a very literal sense that they solved their problem.[34] However, assuming that their behavior is purely instinctive runs counter to such assumptions.

Thus it does not seem obvious at all that in dealing with problems, people generally solve them rationally. But this becomes definitely doubtful when habitual behavior is concerned. I think it can be granted, as a matter of empirical fact, that the regularities which Lewis has in mind are habitual for members of the population. (Rarely instantiated habits are just as reputable as are rarely instantiated regularities.) But the average humans are unlikely to be sufficiently prone to make use of whatever share of rationality they possess, to continuously *solve* their recurrent problems, if this is to be distinguished form behavior which merely avoids them. Most recurring difficulties are escaped by sheer habit; that a habit my be learned does not add to the intelligence which is manifested in displaying it. Rationality may have been manifested in the course of learning; but once habitual, the behavior manifests no more

---

34) This does not mean that intelligence is a matter of inner phenomena of judging, reflecting and the like! Differences in observable behavior can be big enough.

31

rationality than does instinctive behavior. This would be different if problem avoiding habits were usually controlled in the sense that casual failures were met with quick corrections. But everyday experience teaches us a different lesson: Too often, habitual problem avoiding behavior has first to be *broken* in order to allow for useful plasticity in behavior. The more rigid behavior is, the less easily can it be construed as applying solutions to problems.

In the second place, there is no convincing evidence that *expectations* as to what other people will do are really *operative* when we do things which are useful only if other people do certain other things. Such expectations are operative if, when they go wrong, the behavior which they are held responsible for is adjusted. This can frequently be found with new behavior in new situations; therefore it is frequently plausible that new behavior in new situations is actually guided by expectations. But the contrary holds for habitual behavior in recurrent situations; thus, even if present, the expectations are not operative.

Lewis more than once addresses himself to the problem of habitual behavior. He rightly claims that it can be rationally anchored in the agent's preferences and expectations:

"An action may be rational, and may be explained by the agent's beliefs and desires, even though that action was done by habit...A habit may be under the agent's rational control in this sense: If that habit ever ceased to serve the agent's desires according to his beliefs, it would at once be overridden and corrected..."

However, he vastly overstates the extent to which this happens:

"...whatever may be the habitual processes that actually control our choices, if they started tending to go against our beliefs and desires they soon would be overridden, corrected, and retrained..."[35]

In order to get a more adequate view of this matter, we ought to distinguish some points in a possibly continuous scale of repetitive behavior:

(1) Behavior may be repetitive because the same solution is attentively brought about every time. Once the situation were relevantly different, another solution would be found for this situation (i.e. for the first

---

35) 'Languages and Language', pp. 25f., and *Convention*, p. 141. (See also 'Convention: Reply to Jamieson', pp. 114f.) At the close of both passages, I have omitted the words "by conscious reasoning". It would be beside the point ro refute Lewis by pointing out that learning by failure almost never involves conscious reasoning.

situation which is relevantly different). (2) Behavior may be repetitive because the agent relies on his strategy. If a failure were to discredit the strategy, it would be corrected after the first failure (i.e. a new solution would be tried for the second situation which is relevantly different). (3) Behavior may be repetitive because the agent is set in his habit. He reacts to the results of his behavior in the same way in which he reacts to the results of other processes which he has got used to although he could avoid them. Bad results have the effects of mishaps rather than of failures. Many circumstances are relevant for whether or not measures are taken against these mishaps and whether or not such measures consist in changing one's habit; the latter is just one of the possible starting points. Hopefully, the habit may be broken after a good many bad results. (4) Behavior may be repetitive because it is socially sanctioned. The agent is not only set in his habit; the situation he faces is such that his habit counts as unalterable. For him, it is no more among those elements of the situation by which he can control its results.[36)]

Lewis does not require conventional behavior to be socially sanctioned; but he agrees that in fact it will be.[37)] — I submit that behavior of type 1 rationally solves problems and that behavior of type 2 is problem — solving in the sense of being controlled by a problem — solving habit. However, behavior of type 3 is no more problem — solving than, e.g., instinctive behavior, and behavior of type 4 is far beyond anything similar. If it is favorable, it avoids problems; that is all.

Thirdly, since for all members of a modestly large group, it is terribly difficult to pinpoint preferences regarding numerous possible individual actions, construing their behavior as satisfying their *preferences* assumes an air of arbitrariness. This arbitrariness is reduced if[38)] one imputes to all group members a common desire which they all promote by conforming to the regularity in question; most of Lewis' examples are of this sort. This move may be more plausible in some cases than in others. Among car drivers, there is a group — wide desire to avoid collisions, and this group — wide desire is somehow operative in each and every driver (disregarding suicides, and disregarding difficulties with 'operative' for habitual behavior). However, we have no reason to suppose that there is

---

36) If such a situation were construed as a change in the agent's beliefs about what he can do, I should propose to loose interest. There is of course no doubt that, for even the wildest bit of behavior, there is a consistent function which describes it as rational in terms of some beliefs and of some desires.

37) *Convention*, p. 75.

38) — and only if, as Kemmerling has convincingly argued for coordination problems. See *Konvention und sprachliche Kommunikation*, pp. 35—37.

any such group – wide desire, operative in each set of parents, which is achieved by the socially sanctioned parental behavior of bringing up one's children, conservative family ideology notwithstanding. Bringing up one's children has social functions, of course; it secures the expectation of there being people to feed the aged and thereby secures group stability; moreover, it secures survival of offspring, thereby securing group survival. However, none of these goals are operative in many parents, let alone in all. Remember that if 'A's behavior furthers O which is useful for A' is held to suffice for 'A reasonably behaves as he does because he knows that he furthers his goal O in this way', then problem – solving is reduced to problem avoiding.

There is a further, and pretty intricate, problem about behavior satisfying one's preferences, if this behavior is socially sanctioned. Imagine that in a population there exist preferences such that if R were a prevailing regularity in behavior, R would satisfy the preferences about as well as any alternative could do; R, therefore, might possibly become conventional. Let us now compare two different ways for the situation to develop: In the first story, the preferences of several people change (from whatever causes) in such a way that R is no longer a solution to their coordination problem. In the second story, R becomes socially sanctioned. Here the change in preferences occurring in the first story is suppressed precisely because (this is a causal 'because') acting in accordance with them is socially enforced. Now this is quite generally the case — people adjust their preferences to what they are permitted to do. But then the convention sustains preferences rather than satisfying them. Welcoming whatever result one arrives at by some action is quite different from so acting for the sake of it.

§ 13 Choice rules

In order for a regularity in behavior to be conventional in Lewis' sense, it must solve, not only a problem, but a coordination problem: to the regularity in question there must be a viable alternative which would also satisfy the community's members' preferences much better than chaos would. This feature indeed marks Lewis conventions as conventional in a very vivid sense, viz. as a matter of choice. I shall argue that it admits arbitrariness in its application; that it is unclear; and that it unduely restricts what we ought to take into account for present purposes.

Imagine a a group of smokers who seem to conform to the convention of inhaling smoke and using a cigarette – holder. If their common purpose is to go unnoticed when smoking ('Smoke comme il faut!'), then there are alternative fashions, e.g. to keep the smoke in one's mouth and the cigarette between one's lips; thus the regularity may be a convention. If, on the other hand, their common purpose is to create as little air pollution as possible by smoking, then there is no alternative, and the fashion is not conventional. Our possibility of ascertaining that there is an alternative thus depends on finding out the preferences. As we noted in § 12, this will be possible if we assume the relevant preferences to be group – wide; but since it is all too easy to mistake common purpose for social function, finding alternatives will often be a matter of choosing what one takes to be useful for the group – conformative behavior or unpolluted air. Inhaling through a cigarette – holder will be conventional relative to the former purpose only; and there seems to be no sense in deciding which one actually is the group's purpose.

There are cases where this question does not matter because common preferences can plausibly be taken for granted. If they can be satisfied by a regularity different from the one inspected for conventionality, then the former regularity must be available to the group in question. They must, for instance, be capable of changing their behavior:

> "What is not conventional among narrow – minded and inflexible people, who would not know what to do if others began to behave differently, may be conventional among more adaptable people."[39]

Thus behavior which is not accessible because people are too inflexible to do what they could do if they were more flexible does not count as an alternative; from which it seems to follow that what is excluded by the laws of nature is not an alternative either. For instance, walking and its functional analogs like crawling and jumping are not conventional among us because we cannot fly. However, what about alternatives which are excluded by social laws (if there are any)? At present, it seems to be emerging that in a West German type society, even if almost everyone prefers reducing unemployment over the employed working for the unemployed, and even if everyone prefers the means of a general nominal reduction of wages and salaries over that of an inflationary real reduction, coming by the first policy is excluded by something very much like a social law which holds for such societies. The impossibility seems to arise even where all individuals are, in a perfectly good sense, sufficiently adaptable; however, their institutions are not.[40] But would we not

---

39) *Convention*, p. 75.
40) Burge, 'On Knowledge and Convention', p. 254, makes a point which is different in content but similar in thrust: "A second difficulty with the formulation is

like to say that people could act otherwise? Lewis discusses a very similar example[41] of a group whose members would like to change their rules, but where changing is too difficult. He speaks of a convention all the same. This unclarity is no marginal problem; for socially sanctioned behavior is particularly difficult to change.

Finally, in many cases, which I see no reason to exclude from the conventional background of language and where the purpose or function is hardly a matter of dispute and the concept of an alternative presents no difficulty, there simply seem to be no alternatives. For instance, if everybody wants everyone to have an equal chance to catch the bus or to get a ticket to the movies, then there is no alternative to lining up. Is there a point in socially sanctioning such behavior? Not for Lewis:

> "A convention that is *not* arbitrary, so to speak, is a regularity whereby we achieve unique coordination equilibria. Because it is not arbitrary, it does not have to be conventional either. We would conform to it simply because that is the best thing to do. No matter what we had been doing in the past, a failure to conform to the 'nonarbitrary convention' could only be a strategic error (or compensation for someone else's anticipated strategic error, or compensation for someone else's anticipated compensation, etc)."[42]

But people are dull enough to commit strategic errors; so we are well advised to prohibit them from doing so.

§ 14 Knowledge of conventions

In applying Lewis' definition to the Mother – Child example in § 11, I slurred over a margin of imterpretation which opens in his definitions of 'common knowledge' and of 'indicating', especially when these are considered alongside his interpretive remarks and applications to examples. Because the aim of the present considerations is to motivate use of a weaker concept than Lewis' rather than to criticize his concept in its own right, this margin will be characterized in an all – or – nothing manner – in order to show that incorporating common knowledge

---

Continued:
that it presupposes that the participants in a convention *could* switch to an alternative if they believe that the others had done so. But in the case of relatively complicated conventions, the participants might be too set in their ways to learn alternative regularities." (Author's italics.) My point is that the *social apparatus* might be too complicated to allow for changes.

41) *Convention*, p. 92.

42) *Convention*, p. 70 (author's italics).

becomes more interesting for Lewis' concerns the more it exceeds his definitions.

Taken as it stands, the definition requires only that there is evidence, available to every member of the group in question, from which each can rationally conclude (1) that what we termed the convention's 'kernel' holds and (2) that every other member has his evidence too. Whether or not, by using their evidence, they will eventually arrive at knowledge about what others would like to happen if ..., or what they expect each other to do if ..., or what they expect ech other to like to happen if ..., will depend on two steps being taken. They must conclude in a first step, from the evidence at hand, that the 'kernel' holds and that the others have this evidence too; and starting from the facts that the kernel holds and that the others have their evidence too, in a second step, they must arrive at the said bits of actual knowledge. If, by some mishap, they fail to come across such knowledge, then the letter of the definition need not be violated; however, its spirit patently would.

It is even a matter of dispute[43] whether, as Lewis intends his definition to be understood, members of a population could have the required evidence without arriving at actual knowledge; for

> "What $A$ indicates to $x$ will depend...on $x$'s inductive standards and background information."[44]

However, rather than a restriction on the evidence in question, Lewis seems to consider this as a more or less trivial part of the mental equipment of the group members, at least if $A$ consists in past conformity to a regularity in behavior. What they need for the second step, namely

> "mutual ascription of some common inductive standards and background information, rationality, mutual ascription of rationality, and so on"[45]

is not required by the definition (not even in the indirect way just illustrated), and there is no general discussion in *Convention* as to how likely group members are to satisfy such assumptions. However, the whole of pp. 24 to 76 of the book leaves no room for doubt that, in Lewis' view,

---

43) In 'Lewis on Our Knowledge of Conventions', Cooper claims that "Lewis does not distinguish between the case where a person is acquainted with what is in fact evidence for a conclusion, and the case where he is acquaninted with it *as* evidence. Someone may be surrounded by people who regularly do $R$, who expect one another to do it, etc., yet be sublimely unaware of all this." (p. 258, author's italics.)

44) p. 53. I thank Andreas Kemmerling for pointing out that Lewis might intend this sentence as an interpretation rather than as a factual claim.

45) *Convention*, p. 57f.

all but "children and the feeble−minded"[46] are sufficiently rational, have sufficiently high opinions of each others' intelligence, and have enough background information to take the second step.[47] Therefore, even if the definition does not require parties to a convention to know what they are intended to know, it is understood that normal people who satisfy the definition are such that they have the intended knowledge. Considering two extreme interpretations, I shall argue two points: (1) Past conformity does not suffice as a basis of knowledge of conventions; common knowledge as Lewis defines it does not result in what he intends. (2) There is no basis for common knowledge; common knowledge as Lewis intends it does not result from anything like its intended basis. I shall also argue a third point which attacks this idea independently of Lewis' definition: (3) Knowledge of conventions in an everyday sense can exist, but cannot be regarded as a general feature of conventions.

Where 'knowledge' is used in what follows, I agree that one may know something without being just thought about. I do not think that, with non−verbal knowledge, there is a telling difference between knowledge *in sensu composito* and *in sensu diviso*[48] unless knowledge *in sensu diviso* is knowing how in Ryle's sense (on which see below); thus, conceding non−verbal knowledge *in sensu diviso* amounts to no more than conceding knowing how. I do not agree, however, that knowledge may be potential in contrast to actual: if someone only *could* know something but just *does* not, then even if he is in a position to acquire the knowledge, he *has* none so far, be this because he does not make use of available evidence, e.g. in failing to look up in the dictionary which is right before his nose, or because he is too dull or too tired, or because he fails to have opinions which informed people ought to have or has

---

46) p. 62, fn. 1, and p. 75.

47) There is but one indication to the contrary: "[Knowledge of our conventions] may be merely potential knowledge. We must have evidence from which we could reach the conclusion that any of our conventions meets the defining conditions for a convention, but we may not have done the reasoning to reach the conclusion." (p. 63) If 'potential' means 'not arrived at by reasoning', then the sentence fits in with the remainder of the text. However, knowledge which is *based on* evidence may be arrived at without *reasoning from* this evidence, and knowledge, which if existing would be based on available evidence, may be missing for causes other than a failure to reason. If this is what 'potential' means, then the cited passage is strongly inconsistent with the remainder of the text in which Lewis patently takes for granted that in matters of social behavior, people − aside from children and the feeble− minded − believe what they are entitled to believe.

48) See *Convention*, pp. 64−68. Knowledge *in sensu diviso* is all Lewis requires.

opinions which informed people ought not to have. 'Potential knowledge' would be a misleading term for avoidable ignorance. In Cooper's words:

"The expression 'merely potential knowledge'...is scarcely clear, and one's first reaction might be that potential knowledge is no more knowledge than a potential clientele is a clientele. I think first reactions are right."[49]

The argument on point (1) attacks the plausibility of the following prediction: Group members have witnessed passed conformity with $R$ (which satisfies the 'kernel' of convention); therefore, they are likely to know that $R$ is a convention in their group. Argument: The prediction makes use of factual premises on common inductive standards,[50] which are empirically untrustworthy or at least unwarranted. Conclusion: The accessibility of past conformity with $R$ to members of the group is no basis for assuming that they know $R$ to be a convention.

Why are the factual premises dubious? On the level of everyday experience, there is good evidence that different people who have been confronted with past conformity to $R$ will seem to 'witness' different regularities (they interpret the behavior in divergent ways), that their beliefs about what others prefer and are likely to do under different circumstances differ wildly, and that some are more prone than others to rely on their fellows' intelligence, just as some are more likely to be relied upon than others are. Common sense might be considered as a bad source; however, handbook level information about psychological research on social cognition seems to reinforce pessimism: *Information on other people's behavior* is processed in using schemata. Which schema is going to be used may be a matter of chance; once chosen, it becomes self−stabilizing because information is interpreted in accordance with it.[51] Knowledge is gathered only by way of such schemata, which then function in the construction of 'recollections'.[52] Descriptive information

49) 'Lewis on Our Knowledge of Conventions', p. 256. The aim of Cooper's argument differs from mine; he tries to show that if the definition is satisfied, then people know their convention in a full−blooded sense of 'know'. He remarks (*ibid.*) that this result tends to narrow the extension of the concept of convention, if compared to Lewis' "poor sort of knowledge"; however, he does not venture a guess as to how widespread full−blooded knowledge of conventions, and thus the existence of Lewis conventions, might in fact be.

50) I apologize for being no more explicit on the premises' precise formulation than Lewis is. The argument is that no sufficiently strong assumptions hold good.

51) Wyer and Gordon, in: *Handbook of Social Cognition*, ed. by R.S. Wyer and Th.K. Srull, Erlbaum, Hillsdale/ N.J., and London, 1984, Vol. 2, pp. 75f.

52) Wyer and Gordon, *l.c.*, pp. 99f.; Hastie, Park, and Weber, *l.c.*, p. 190.

which is incompatible with expectations is forgotten quicker than schema — consistent descriptive information.[53] An observer uses information on other people's behavior better the easier it fits in with a plan — goal — schema which happens to be available to him.[54] Further distortions enter into the perception of group behavior: Behavior of people is perceived as more similar if they are perceived as forming a group, and such regularities need not be exaggerated but can be completely fictional.[55] The simple fact that people are reckoned with the observer's own group distorts his perception of their behavior in an evaluatively positive way;[56] one might expect that preference attributions to members of one's own group are similarly distorted. In sum, then, science does not seem to contradict a down — to — earth view of how people arrive at their opinions about each other.

Now the very untrustworthiness of the ancillary premises is crucial for the argument on point (2). The above prediction of knowledge is an indirect argument: Given certain information, we are expected without further investigation to rely on conventions being known. In contrast, one may think of a direct argument: The members of the group in question present a peculiar appearance which can best be understood on the assumption that they have common knowledge of their conventions which is based on evidence about everyone's past behavior. Whatever this peculiar appearance may be, it must consist of facts about the group members' behavior which are best interpreted as manifesting knowledge which is actually based on that evidence. It will not actually be so based (in contrast to warranted), unless the above ancillary premises refer to dispositions which the group members really have. Since we have no reason to assume they do, we cannot regard such an interpretation as the best one. (Inferences to $p$ as the best explanation of $q$ depend on the plausibility of the further premises which are needed in the explanation.)

The difference which should be stressed between some knowledge being actually based on bits of evidence and its being warranted by this evidence might become more translucent if we point out that knowledge need not even be actually based on the data the initial reception of which was once responsible for acquiring the relevant beliefs. It seems appropriate to add this remark here, because Lewis might possibly like to view his basis for common knowledge as a starting point in a learning process.

53) Wyer and Gordon, l.c., pp. 125 − 129, 136.
54) Wyer and Gordon, l.c., p. 105.
55) Hamilton, in Cognition and Social Behavior, ed. by J.S. Carrol and J.W. Payne, Erlbaum, Hillsdale, N.J., 1975, pp. 85 − 87, 92.
56) Hamilton, l.c., p. 84; Hastie, Park, and Weber, l.c., p. 180f.

Compare the following passage (the verbal/nonverbal question is not relevant for the present context):

"Like it or not, we have plenty of knowledge we cannot put into words. And plenty of our knowledge, in words or not, is based on evidence we cannot hope to report. Our beliefs are formed under the influence of impressions left by a body of past experiences, but it is only occcasionally that these impressions allow us to report the experience that created them. You probably believe that Kamchatka exists. Your belief is justified, for it is based on evidence: mostly your exposure to various books and to incidents that confirm the reliability of such books. Try, then, to make a convincing case for the existence of Kamchatka by reporting parts of your experinece. There is no reson why our knowledge of our conventions should be especially privileged. Like any other knowledge we have, it can be tacit, or based on tacitly known evidence, or both."[57]

I fully agree that most of our knowledge is nonverbal. However, if Lewis speaks of 'tacitly known evidence' and 'evidence we cannot hope to report', and if he equates 'based on evidence' with 'formed under the influence of impressions left by a body of past experiences' which 'created' the impressions, he is obviously stretching the relation of *evidence which justifies belief* so far as to cover *experiences which cause belief*.[58] In short, he interprets *having learned that p* as *having evidence for p* or, as in the rowing case,[59] *perceiving that p* as *having evidence for p*. However, learning is a process which causally creates our knowledge; any different process with the same effect would do just as well. Whether or not our knowledge is justified by our learning data is thus at best of accidental interest for its base. Whether or not it is actually so based depends, for instance, on whether or not new data, which would have cut off the learning process if it had been among the learning data, would lead us to change our minds if we were now confronted with it. This is anything but obvious.

The general idea of common knowledge of conventions, or at least that of knowledge of them, might to a certain extent be saved if we drop the requirement that it be based on particular evidence in a certain way. Let us therefore turn to point (3) and ask: Do people generally know their conventions, however based their knowledge may be? In order to avoid

---

57) *Convention*, p. 64.
58) Lewis is not alone in doing so, of course; more or less causal accounts of knowledge are the fashion of the day. Fashions pass.
59) *Convention*, p. 63.

difficulties about which definition of convention is to underlie our question, let us resort to a minimum: Do people generally know many of the sorts of behavior which are sanctioned among them?

In one sense they do: They know how to behave, for this is just a way of expressing that they behave in the ways which are sanctioned in their group. However, we must not be misled by the suggestiveness of the following chain of reformulations:

*behaving correctly*
knowing how to behave
knowing how one has to behave
knowing the correct behavioral patterns
knowing which behavioral patterns are correct behavioral patterns
knowing what *behaving correctly* consists in

Kemmerling[60] suggests that Lewis hovers between knowing how and knowing that, and he rightly remarks that knowing how would not do justice to Lewis' manifest idea that knowledge of convention should, for rational agents, justify conformative behavior. In order to betray interesting knowledge of socially sanctioned behavior, agents who know their behavior to be correct, should differ in behavior from agents who do not; still the difference must make sense for nonverbal knowledge.

Let us look at sample differences which, even if consisting of verbal behavior, make sense for nonverbal knowledge of one's socially sanctioned behavior. Somebody who not only is a member of a group which follows $R$, but also (even if nonverbally) knows that $R$ is followed, is prepared (1) to fight for the replacement of $R$ with $R'$ if he prefers $R'$ over $R$, and (2) to fight for the propagation of $R$ in other groups, if he wishes all groups to follow his own group's conventions. However, for too many people and regularities, neither (1) nor (2) are actually exhibited. People who sincerely prefer equal rights for women fail to fight for emancipation because they wrongly believe that discrimination is not conventional. University professors sincerely propagate the principle of achievement as a mechanism for vocational selection because they wrongly believe that it is a rule, worthy of emulating, which they themselves observe (instead of the principle that you scratch my back and I'll scratch yours). In short, one wide—spread cause for people's ignorance

---

60) *Konvention und sprachliche Kommunikation*, p. 27f. In 'Languages and Language', p. 25, Lewis states a condition, sufficient for knowledge of conventions, which reads like a definition of knowing how: "It is enough to be able to recognize conformity and non—conformity to his convention, and to be able to try to conform to it."

of their conventions consists in the fact that actual conventions tend to diverge from ideologies.

Now, if it is not knowledge — let alone rationally acquired rational expectations — that launches and stabilizes even our useful sanctioned behavior, then what else could explain this miracle of nature? I have no competent opinion.[61] The theory of origin and conservation of social stability is beyond the professional limits of a philosopher. In analyzing concepts, philosophers may indeed betray their liking for a picture of human nature: they reserve the right for man, viewed in a certain way, to satisfy the requirements which they lay down in their analysis of an essentially human feature. I think we ought neither to exclude nor to be afraid of the idea that behavior among humans comes to be and remains socially sanctioned in ways which resemble those of other gregarious animals. Man is not an *animal sociale* by virtue of being an *animal rationale*: it may well be that being social is more fundamental than rationality.

§ 15 Can meaning sneak in via common knowledge?

What is common knowledge good for in a definition of convention? If we do not care about the exact definition of 'common knowledge' but consider the ideas which are evoked by words like 'know', then we would feel that group members who share common knowledge of the kernel of their conventions solve their coordination problems in an extra — rational way: They know they have a coordination problem, they know why it is one, and their expectations (in which light their behavior is rational anyway) are warranted by what they know. This is a pleasing view for philosophers who think that man is a rational animal. With Lewis, however, there are more practical uses of common knowledge. A minor sevice of the condition is that some unwelcome examples are excluded;[62] the major one is the bridge it builds from convention to meaning. Lewis tries to prove that a speaker who utters a sign in accordance with a convention of language[63] *thereby* means the conventional meaning of that sign; in his proof, common knowledge plays an essential part.

---

61) Even if my bias is more on Burge's side: "The stability of conventions is safeguarded not only by enlightened self — interest, but by inertia, superstition, and ignorance." ('On Knowledge and Convention', p. 253.)

62) *Convention*, pp. 53ff., 59.

63) *Convention*, pp. 154 — 159. The proof is carried out for a primitive form of linguistic conventions, viz. signalling conventions, but Lewis conjectures that the result is generalizable (p. 159).

This, of course, is a delightful result. If what we normally regard as linguistic utterances can be shown to be actions by which the speaker means something thanks to the fact that he sticks to a convention, then we seem to gain a deep insight into what the meaningfulness of language owes to its conventionality.

All well and good — if by independent reasons common knowledge can be shown to be a feature of conventions which govern linguistic behavior. I have tried to show in § 14 that, in the sense of (nonverbal, latent, but:) actual knowledge, it is a very improbable feature of human behavior; and it is precisely this sense in which common knowledge is required for Lewis' proof. To show this, I shall examine one detail.

Lewis tries to prove that the speaker's doing σ (signalling) after observing s, upon observing which the audience conventionally responds by r, is covered by the three Gricean intentions for his meaning nonnaturally that the audience should respond by r, and that it is covered by the second intention in particular, viz. the speaker's intention that his audience recognize the speaker's intention to produce r by doing σ. Here is his proof ("I" is the speaker, "you" his audience):

> "I expect you to infer s upon observing that I do σ. I expect you to recognize my desire to produce r, conditionally upon s. I expect you to recognize my expectation that I can produce r by doing σ. So I expect you to recognize my intention to produce r, when you observe that I do σ."[64]

The second and third premises are to be previded by common knowledge (the first one is in the kernel). They require actual expectations;[65] merely being entitled to expectations would not suffice for actually having intentions. Even if Lewis were right in saying:

> "The intention with which I do σ can be established by examinaing the practical reasoning that justifies me in doing it. I need not actual-

64) *Convention*, p. 155.
65) Actual in the sense of real rather than occurrent. Actual expectations are dispositions too. On *p.* 9 of *Languages and Language*, Lewis suggests: "Perhaps a negative version of [common knowledge] would do the job: no one believes that others disbelieve this, and so on." Applied the above proof, this would yield something like the following: I do not question that you might infer s upon observing that i do σ; I do not question that you recognize my desire to produce r, conditional upon s; I do not question that you might recognize that I put up with producing r by doing σ. Whether or not what follows from this would suffice in the context of remodelled Gricean conditions (cp. fn. 94), I do not know.

ly go through that reasoning to have an intention; actions done without deliberations are often done with definite intentions", [66]

we ought not to conclude that, because thinking something out is more than is required for thoughtful behavior, being entitled to believe something could substitute for believing it. Where belief is required for intentions, availability of evidence will not do in its place. [67] Consider the following sequence:

In every instance of *S*, *x* has *witnessed* that *p*.
In every instance of *S*, *x* has *noticed* that *p*.
Of every instance of *S*, *x knows* that *p*.
In every instance of *S*, *x expects* that *p*.

Take any of its steps, and it will make sense to claim that many people frequently fail to take it. However, since each of the four words leave room for interpretation, an *unexpecting witness* can hardly be described as having failed to take exactly one of the steps (rather than another). Thus the feeling arises that the break in the sequence is not real, the connection still potential. (Every heap is potentially a void place.) Perhaps this elusiveness extends, via intending, to meaning. That nonnatural meaning exists, by and large, only potentially I am the last sceptic to doubt. [68]

I conclude that, if defined as availability of evidence, common knowledge cannot play the part of importing meaning via convention; actual common knowledge might suffice, but is unlikely to exist. This motive for incorporating it in a definition of convention is void.

§ 16 Conventional make – ups and how to detect them

As we shall see in the course of our investigations, conventional facts which are immediately relevant for linguistic meaning rarely consist in the group's requiring or prohibiting of some simple behavioral patterns. However, the relevant conventional facts can be interpreted in such a way that they are ultimately established by reference to rather simple requiring and prohibiting rules. I shall now try to show this for the conventional

---

66) *Convention*, p. 155.
67) The same assumption of actual beliefs (in contrast to one's being entitled to believe) is used in Bennett's parallel argument in *Linguistic Behaviour*, p. 180: (The speaker) "utters *S* intending to communicate *P*, and expecting to succeed only *because he thinks that A* will think that he utters *S* with that intention; which means that he is relying upon *A*'s recognizing what his intention is...". (Italics mine.)
68) Independent arguments against speakers' making their utterances with the second Gricean intention are given in § 31.

situations which I need in the analysis of my case study. This rather tedious business will be strictly confined to items which are actually used, as can be seen from a quick glance at Appendix I and II.

The word 'conventional situation' is not very apt. I need a term which covers all conventional features which together characterize what is conventional about a situation, and I shall use the expression 'conventional make−up'. Situations may lack a conventional make−up; nobody has any conventionally guaranteed expectations, for example. Other situations have conventional make−ups. For instance, when I am about to cross the road, I am expected to heed traffic, and car drivers are expected to pay attention to what I do. Thus both parties are conventionally committed to certain dispositions, and the fact that they are committed in this way belongs to the conventional make−up of the situation.

Sometimes the conventional make−up of a situation which is characteristically connected with a given utterance meaning will impose relative obligations. There will be an obligation to do one thing rather than a certain other thing, without there being an absolute obligation to do the first. That is to say, if the agent has to choose between them, he must opt for the first: In a certain situation he is more obligated to do the first than he is to do the second. The same relation may obtain between different agents: In a given situation, one may be more obligated than the other to do a certain thing. Finally, one and the same person may be more obligated to do one and the same thing in one situation than he would be in another. (This is frequently the case with language: obligations may increase because the situation has been modified by the occurrence of an utterance.)

I shall now propose a certain way of connecting these and other concepts through a network of definitions. My starting point is an undefined six−place predicate; the chain of definitions will lead to some three− and four−place predicates. We shall use all but the undefined primitive. Knitting the definitional net will hopefully show which conventional make−ups are empirically more directly accessible than others, and how the empirical applicability of the latter profits from their connection with the former. In general, the defined predicates are easier to apply empirically than those which are used to define them. I shall use '$x$', '$y$' for agents, '$s$', '$t$' for situations, '$u$', '$v$' for actions. The primitive predicate is:

In $s$, $x$ is more obligated to do $u$ than $y$ is to do $v$ in $t$.

This predicate would be straightforwardly intelligible if we could operate with degrees of obligation. The intuitive idea is that there are such degrees; but we do not need them in what follows. For comparing one

46

agent's obligations vis à vis different actions in different situations, or two agents' obligations vis à vis the same action in different situations, or two agents' obligations vis à vis different actions in the same situation, we get three five − place predicates (formally, by identifying the respective variables in the primitive predicate):

In $s$, $x$ is more obligated to do $u$ than he is to do $v$ in $t$.

In $s$, $x$ is more obligated to do $u$ than $y$ is to do it in $t$.

In $s$, $x$ is more obligated to do $u$ than $y$ is to do $v$.

For comparing only the obligations either of two persons or vis à vis two actions or in two situations, by the same formal procedure we get:

In $s$, $x$ is more obligated to do $u$ than $y$ is.

In $s$, $x$ is more obligated to do $u$ than he is to do $v$.

In $s$, $x$ is more obligated to do $u$ than he is in $t$.

In the case of these four − place predicates, there can be good evidential support for their application. That in $s$, $x$ is more obligated to do $u$ than he is in $t$, can be confirmed, for classes of cases where $x$ can choose between the same alternatives to $u$, by the following observations: $u$ is chosen more often in $s$ than it is chosen in $t$; omitting $u$ in $s$ makes $x$ more liable to more severe sanctions than it does in $t$; and sanctions are ore readily accepted in $s$ than they are in $t$. That in $s$, $x$ is more obligated to do $u$ than $y$ is, can be confirmed, for constant pairs of agents, by the following observations: $x$ does $u$ more often than $y$; if both omit $u$, $x$ becomes more liable to more severe sanctions; if both omit $u$ and if both are punished, $y$ is more prone to reject the sanctions. That in $s$, $x$ is more obligated to do $u$ than to do $v$, can be confirmed by the following observations, if $s$ is always the same situation: $u$ is chosen more often than is $v$; the choice of $v$ makes $x$ more liable to more severe sanctions; sanctions for doing $v$ are more readily accepted than sanctions for doing $u$.

That $x$ is obligated, in an absolute sense, to do $u$ in $s$ can be defined in the following way:

If $x$ cannot do both $u$ and $v$ in $s$, then in $s$ $x$ is more obligated to do $u$ than he is to do $v$.

This means that $x$ is more obligated to do $u$ than he is to do anything incompatible with it; and it means that $x$ actually is positively obligated because omitting $u$ is incompatible with $u$.

Whence can we gather empirical evidence for the five − place predicates to obtain? One way, of course, would consist in collecting evidence in the same way as before. Take, as an example, the question whether or not $x$ is more obligated to do $u$ in $s$ than he is to do $v$ in $t$. We can try to find this out by switching $x$ from $s$ where he did $u$ or omitted it, to $t$ where he does $v$ or omits it, and by comparing the reactions which result. But this brings to the surface a tacit assumption which we also had to make above: We must rely on situations and behaviors remaining identical in all relevant aspects; i.e. we are tacitly assuming the validity of *social laws* which say what it is about people, situations and behavioral patterns, that is relevant for the obligations of agents. To illustrate this, let me design an artificial example. We suspect that in the group under consideration, male individuals are *ceteris paribus* more obligated to manifest effort than are female individuals. (The example is artificial.) That is, we suspect that the following law is valid within the group:

(1) If $s$ and $t$ are completely symmetrical, with respect to gains and losses, when $x$ does $u$ in $s$ and $y$ does $v$ in $t$, and if $x$ is male and $y$ female, then in $s$, $x$ is more obligated to do $u$ than $y$ is to do $v$ in $t$.

From this putative law, the following one can be derived for a situation $s$ in which both $x$ and $y$ are involved; it may then be a good deal easier to judge the symmetry:

(2) If $s$ is completely symmetrical, with respect to gains and losses, when $x$ does $u$ in $s$ and $y$ does $v$ in $s$, and if $x$ is male and $y$ female, then in $s$, $x$ is more obligated to do $u$ than $y$ is to do $v$.

We may think of the difference in social pressure on a man to offer his seat to an older person and that on a woman to remain standing for the benefit of an older person. – Consider next a man, $x$, in a situation $s$ which is such that both $x$ and some woman want to enter through a door which cannot be entered throught simultaneously. Then from (2), with help of this description of $s$, we get:

(3) If a man wants to enter through a door at the same time as some woman, and if it is not possible for them to enter through simultaneously, then he is more obligated to enter after her than he is to enter before her.

Finally, since in this situation, entering before and after her are incompatible, we get:

(4) If a man, $x$, is in a situation $s$ such that he wants to enter through a door at the same time as a woman, but both cannot enter through simultaneously, then he has to let her pass first.

This is confirmable by the weak Hart analysis. If many laws like this follow from (3), then (3) is confirmable not only in the manner sketched above, but also by the derivability of (4); and so are (2) and (1) if many laws descend from every theoretical story. (1) imparts such confirmation to all of its consequences, and in particular to those consequences which predict conventional make – ups characterized by the rest of our five –

and four — place predicates. As soon as we have a good theory of the group's conventional behavior, these conventional make — ups, then, are empirically accessible from two directions.

Let us note one important feature about the conventional make — up of any particular situation: The make — up is never studied with special attention, let alone exclusive attention, to this very situation. The question as to whether or not the situation has a certain conventional make — up is answered according to whether or not there is a well — confirmed law which states that, for some bundle $F$ of features which characterize the situation under consideration, the reactions and dispositions which have to be expected if a situation has the conventional make — up in question, actually turn up in all situations which share $F$. This fact makes conventional make — ups of situations more easily accessible (although indirectly accessible) than any individual agents' intentions. The statistical laws which need to be established indiscriminately refer to every group member and provide, therefore, a larger basis for confirmation than statistical laws about single persons ever could.

Some further concepts will be used later on: Equal strength of obligation, either in $s$ and $t$ or vis à vis $u$ and $v$ or of $x$ and $y$, can be defined by negating stronger obligations in both directions. Being more permitted (being more entitled, having a stronger claim), either in $s$ as compared to $t$, or as of $x$ as compared to $y$, or to do $u$ as compared to $v$, can be defined as being less obligated to omit. We shall also need a concept of absolute permission. According to the intuitions which I shall rely upon, this concept will have to be a rather strong one. What is permitted must not simply fail to be prohibited; group members must be prohibited to apply sanctions to the aagent for doing what he is permitted to do. Therefore, that $x$ is permitted to do $u$ in $s$ means that group members are obligated not to apply sanctions to $x$ for doing $u$ in $s$.

We cannot expect a group's system of rules to conform to every desirable consistency standard. However, if we describe behavioral patterns as prohibited or as permitted in a group, our descriptive concepts should satisfy some conditions of adequacy. Let me state three:

(1) If $x$ is obligated to do $u$ in $s$, then $x$ is not obligated to omit $u$ in $s$.
(2) If $x$ is permitted to omit $u$ in $s$, then $x$ is not obligated to do $u$ in $s$.
(3) If $x$ is permitted to do $u$ in $s$, then $x$ is not obligated to omit $u$ in $s$.

Using the weak Hart analysis and our definition of being permitted, we can informally prove that the three conditions hold. (1) holds simply because not both $u$ and omitting $u$ can be general in $s$. As to (2): If $x$ is permitted to omit $u$ in $s$, then everyone is obligated not to apply sanctions to $x$ for omitting $u$ in $s$; therefore, $x$ is not obligated to do $u$ in $s$. As to (3): If $x$ is permitted to do $u$ in $s$, then everyone is obligated not to apply sanctions to $x$ for doing $u$ in $s$. Then in general, nobody applies such sanctions; therefore, $x$ is not obligated to omit $u$ in $s$.

Note that the inverse of neither (2) nor (3) holds. If $x$ is not permitted to omit $u$, it may all the same be the case that he is not obligated to do $u$; if he is not obligated to omit it, he may all the same not be permitted to do it. There is room for actions such that the group neither enforces their omission nor protects their performance, as well as for actions such that the group neither protects their omission nor enforces their performance. It doesn't even follow from the definitions that $x$ is permitted to do what he is obligated to do. The definitions entail that if $x$ is obligated to do $u$, then $x$'s doing $u$ will in general not meet with sanctions from any group member (because his omitting $u$ would be exposed to sanctions, and if doing $u$ were exposed to sanctions too, sanctions could not be released by either doing or omitting $u$, but by something else). However, if some group member all the same applies a sanction to $x$ for doing $u$, then although $x$ himself will, in general, not tolerate it, defending himself may be left up to him.

At one place, we shall also need the idea that whether or not he does $u$ is someone's own business; this means that he is permitted to do it and permitted to omit it. Furthermore, there will be some conventional make−ups which are more complicated; the first one I cannot define, but can only interpret incompletely:

If in $t$, $x$ shares more responsibility for consequences of $u$ than he does in $s$, then

(1) if $x$'s obligations to partake in compensating for consequences of $u$ are of equal strength in $s$ and $t$, then in $t$ he has to compensate for more of the damage than in $s$; and

(2) if $x$ has to compensate for the same amount of damage in $s$ as in $t$, then his obligation to do so is stronger in $t$ than in $s$.

In a parallel fashion, this analysis applies to a difference in responsibility between $x$ and $y$ in one situation (instead of between $s$ and $t$ for one $x$).

I am not completely certain about a concept which occurs e.g. in the conventional result of apologizing, namely that '$x$ is (not) liable for compensating $y$ for $u$'; it might be construed as an unconditional obligation or as an obligation which arises only upon $u$'s request. Someone's being less liable for compensation ought to be interpreted by a combination of liability and the explanation above of a bigger share in responsibility.

Being in no way responsible for consequences of $v$ will occur too; this means not being obligated to compensate for any damage which results from $v$.

A conventional make−up which is fundamental for constatives is that at $x$'s expense, $y$ can rely on $p$ obtaining; this means that $x$ is liable for compensating all damage which results for $y$ from $y$'s erroneously relying on the fact that $p$. That $x$ is individually responsible for the consequences of $v$ means that if $y$ ($\neq x$) is damaged by $v$, then $x$ and no one else is liable for compensation. − The last remark is on being forced to do something and merits its own definition:

> '$u$ is imposed on $x$ by $y$'s doing $v$' for 'there are things, which $x$ can do and which would prevent consequences of $y$'s behavior $v$, consequences such that $x$ is permitted to perform at least one action which prevents them, and none of these things is $x$ more permitted to do than $u$'.

That is, $u$ is a maximally and positively permitted way for $x$ to escape untolerable consequences of $v$.

This, then concludes my sketch of how the conventional make−ups of situations which will play a crucial role in my case study are to be interpreted and tested empirically. I am fully aware that important gaps remain. As noted above, I did not attempt to clarify the concepts underlying that of a sanction; a related omission consists in my failing to clarify the concepts of damage and compensation, which play a prominent role in a good part of this section. I agree that this distracts from what I can claim to achieve in the chapters which follow.

The conventional make−ups considered so far are not particularly linguistic in character. This is no accident. I do not think that there are conventional make−ups (like 'You are obligated to make only true statements'), identifiable all over the world, which are peculiar to linguistic conventions. In my view, meaningful utterances only bring about changes in conventional make−ups which are pre−linguistically determined. This view opens up a wide prospect about different things which might be termed linguistic conventions, or linguistic rules. The very last section of the present book shall be dedicated to this question.

# Chapter III
# A case for utterance meaning: NIVEAU zero

## § 17 A plea for case studies

I shall now go on to explain and defend my approach in an extra lengthy, long – winded, and admittedly, not very highfalutin' way, viz. in inquiring whether or not a certain empirical system of conventions constitutes a language (or has a language embedded in it). There are, of course, at least two further approaches to clarifying concepts – pictured as extremes, but intelligibly enough. The first consists of designing a system of rules, definitions, conditions of adequacy and considerations why the latter are satisfied, etc. etc., with at best cursory allusions to fragments of examples. The intended field of application of such analyses is not completely clear in every case; and as a rule they fail to convince anyone that they have a chance of producing reasonable results if applied to concrete problems. The second approach consists in applying a proposed analysis to constructed examples. There is a great advantage in this. We learn roughly what it is that matters for the analysis to be fruitful. However, there is an obvious weakness in it, viz. the risk of the example being trimmed to fit the proposed analysis. We forfeit the opportunity of learning from unforeseen problems, of improving our analysis, perhaps even of changing its fundamental approach.

This is as an opportunity we can hope to exploit if we develop our analysis through applying it to an empirical case, i.e. to a language which is actually used by some community, a language which we are able to get a hold on in a way that would justify our hope of distinguishing, on the one hand, between results that hold only for fragments which were cleverly chosen, and, on the other hand, results which have a chance of remaining probable when more evidence is adduced.

I shall study a case which is hopefully easily accessible to most readers, because they can readily frame a coherent conception of the relevant facts, provided they possess a driver's license (and can swiftly shift their imagination from right to left and left to right if they are British). The system of conventions which will be inspected for language use comprises the rules followed by drivers in West Germany; the system's prima facie function seems to consist in helping everyone to drive quickly but safely. It might be useful to warn at least American readers that though West Germany is not exactly like Italy, we do in fact take some risks, have more respect for radar traps than for speed limits, find it boring to remain in one lane, and have difficulties in appreciating a big Mercedes overtaking a slow truck with a 20 km/h difference while all our Volkswagens are lined up behind him in the passing lane. Though traffic rules mean a great deal to us, our behavior leaves room for the beneficial workings of additional rules which determine our mutual expectations as to reasonable ways of applying the traffic rules. Most official rules form part of the system of implicit rules in one form or other; but I am interested exclusively in implicit rules, and in official ones only insofar as they are implicit ones. (The interplay between official and implicit rules may be complicated; but learning the system in driving is quite easy.)

The main reason for choosing this system for the present inquiry was that it is comparatively small. As the definition of utterance meaning in § 24 will show, the present approach is holistic: the attribution of meaning to any single utterance is derived from a theory which in an unequalled way describes the whole of the community's conventional system. Now we may believe it or not that if two rival theories both claim to achieve this, there will be disciplined ways of balancing their respective merits and disadvantages; this is because there exists no 'scientific community' for describing the ways in which utterance meanings depend on situations, no persevering, cooperative endeavor of people who really care about what speakers are committed to have said in using certain sentences under such and such circumstances. Scientific communities have established their standards for inquiring into the meanings of sentences at least since the first grammarians turned to systematic translation; virtually nobody, however, has colleagues with whom he regularly discusses what a speaker says in uttering "Fine, isn't it?", depending on the context, or why semantical inexplicitness, far from being a performance mistake, does not disturb everyday conversation in any signigficant way − i.e. how the context substitutes for the contribution of semantics (or vice versa).

Thus I cannot presuppose that the reader would grant that one can reasonably weigh theories about when and why it is useful to posit utterance meanings; this is why I have to demonstrate how I fancy this to be done, in order to convince the reader that it is possible. And this in turn has forced me to choose, as my demonstration model, a system which is poor enough to be described as a whole.

The most salient consequence is that I had to use a system without syntax. There is simply no use for syntax in poor natural systems of communication − be it only because handling twenty signs by heart is easier than using four elementary signs and one commutation rule. Therefore, with the results of my case study, I am not entitled to say anything that involves either sentence structure or subsentential expressions.

There is, however, no real disadvantage in this. For my three steps outlined in § 7 are independent of each other. One may accept the analysis of conventional facts in chapter II while refusing the analysis of utterance meaning in the present and the next chapters, and vice versa. Or one may be impressed by the view on sentence meaning in chapters VI and VII while rejecting both the views on conventional facts and on utterance meaning, etc. Since there exist sophisticated theories on matters semantical, there would be no use in adding an incompetent additional theory about how meanings of sentences depend on their structures and on the meanings of their parts. It is quite sufficient, and perhaps even too much, to propose a theory about how the sentence meaning ascriptions resulting from advanced semantic theories are to be tested empirically. For this purpose, my case study is indeed intended to be helpful; for on its basis, I can argue for a way of checking sentence meaning hypotheses insofar as this is possible to do while disregarding structural information.

West German car drivers use a signalling system (which is called 'NIVEAU', short for 'NIcht−VErbale AUtofahrersprache'),[70] and they can say indefinitely many things in using it. It resembles natural languages in being free from any legislation, in developing continually, and in being learnt in use like a native tongue. Withholding from it the title of language can have but two deplorably misguided motives. The first one is that language needs syntax because otherwise there could be no new signs to utter (which is a half−truth, though I admit that it has got the better half) and, consequently, no new things to say − one of the falsest opinions of many I know, one that displays a deep misunderstanding of how a speaker manages to say something. I shall return to this question in § 26. The second motive is that speaking ought to work by using one's larynx, palate, tongue, teeth, and lips, or at least other parts of one's own body; to this I shall neither reply nor return. Pre−theoretically, the West German car drivers' signalling system is a natural language, except for syntax and bodily articulation; therefore, it is a natural language.

There is a dangerous idea, however, that might induce us to turn away from traffic if we want to look for language. Isn't language a medium that is to be used to speak about the world; to communicate on nature,

---

70) It has been described for the general reader (and with many nice, pre−theoretical pictures) in my *Die Signalsprache der Autofahrer*.

essence, morality, on the heavens, the stars, and the gods? Does anything like this happen between drivers when they are signalling? Well, no, in fact it does not. And in partly answering this objection, I must appeal to the reader's patience: We shall eventually meet with people uttering statements of fact. On the other hand, there will be no specific analysis of statements on eternal truths, or on truths about eternal entities, simply because that would be the wrong order. I do not know of arguments that tend or purport to prove that there might be people, or groups of people, who are used to talking about elevated matters without, occasionally, talking about more elementary things, or even about nothing, while cleaning dishes, digging ditches, ploughing, cooking, repairing shoes and faucets. Rather, there is almost any degree of plausibility that those people who do highbrow talking must from time to time converse while doing more down − to − earth things.

And then it is at least not unreasonable to rely, in inquiring whether a given group is using a language, on a procedure that is more fruitful if that group uses only a humble everyday language rather than a noble scientific one, and, in developing this procedure, to proceed by first applying it to some such humble case. This is not to claim that if the procedure is shown to work fairly well in humble cases it is thereby shown to be fruitful in analyzing the language of physics, of mathematics, or of theology, or even to answer any question we could ask about humble languages. I am convinced it is fruitful in these respects too; but I cannot, and I shall not try to, argue my conviction.

## § 18 The first utterance meaning rules

As any didactic drama condenses life, my performance gathers many relevant results from a lengthy analysis and packs them into an artificial sequence of discoveries.

*Step 1*: Some *background conventions* are collected which are central to drivers' business, viz. the complete set of anti − collision norms. They state which one of two drivers has to wait, to slow down, or to move out of the way if they are to otherwise risk a collision; we say that the second then 'ranks before' the first.

(BC 1) $x$ is driving in his right lane, while $y$ is driving in his left lane; then $x$ ranks before $y$.

(BC 2) $x$ is on a public road, while $y$ is not; then $x$ ranks before $y$.

(BC 3) $x$ is in flowing traffic, $y$ in stationary traffic; then $x$ ranks before $y$.

(BC 4) $x$ is driving forward, $y$ backward; then $x$ ranks before $y$.

(BC 5) $x$ is driving on a main road, $y$ on a side road; then $x$ ranks before $y$.[71]

(BC 6) From the point of view of $y$, $x$ comes from the right; then $x$ ranks before $y$.

(BC 7) $y$ is about to turn left, $x$ approaches from the opposite direction; then $x$ ranks before $y$.

(BC 8) $x$ keeps his lane, $y$ changes his lane; then $x$ ranks before $y$.

In cases where two rules have incompatible results, the rule with the lower number ranks higher.[72] — Note that the background conventions do not refer to any party to the situation uttering anything. (BC 1) to (BC 8) prevent every possible collision but one (the rare case of four cars simultaneously arriving at a non—regulated cross—roads), and since avoiding collisions is imperative for drivers, this body of conventions is as functional as one could wish. Our description of the group's conventions leaves it intact; this is an achievement which counts in the description's favor.

*Step 2*: To the anti—collision norms, we find exceptions of the following kind: In cases where $x$ should rank before $y$ according to the anti—collision norms, sometimes $x$ not only is permitted to go on, but even ought to do so — '$x$ is due before $y$'; sometimes $y$ ranks before $x$; and sometimes even $y$ is due before $x$. The exceptions are tentatively construed as due to the hypothetical fact that as yet undiscovered utterances with certain meanings have, by virtue of their conventional results, changed the background conventional situation. The knowledge to be used for this interpretation is stated in the following *explications of utterance meanings* ('PC' is short for 'precondition' — the explications

---

71) To avoid any suspicion of circularity, I am adding definitions: At junctions or crossroads, a main road is defined by any one of the signs 301, 306, or 330, a side road by any one of the signs 205 or 206 of the "Straßenverkehrsordnung".

72) I am neglecting traffic regulation by policemen or traffic lights. — Let me make two points regarding (BC 1) to (BC 8): I do not claim to correctly describe the legal situation but rather the rules actually complied with by drivers (both may be hopefully identical). Furthermore, my description is not likely to be empirically more correct than is necessary for present purposes. I have doubts, for instance, about the universal empirical validity of (BC 6) — "Rechts vor Links" — at junctions which are not crossings, because I do not know whether or not the frequent deviations by drivers who come from the left and are driving in the straight road are generally accepted as natural. Similar doubts arise when $x$ is a cyclist and $y$ a car driver. Such uncertainties are not critical for our case study, however, because revising them would lead to more rules, or more complicated ones, which would be affected by the following modifications in just the same way; and it is the modifications that matter.

are conditional, and therefore only partial —, 'UM' for 'utterance meaning', 'CR' for 'conventional result'):

($\alpha$) (PC) By failing to do $U$, [73] $x$ prevents $y$ from doing $V$. $x$ is more entitled to omit doing $U$ than $y$ is to do $V$. (UM) Now $x$ *insists* to $y$ on omitting $U$. Then (CR) $x$ has to omit $U$ (and, in our story, $x$ *is due before $y$*); $y$ has to omit $V$; and $x$ comes to share more responsibility than before for the consequences of $V$'s being left undone.

($\beta$) (PC) By failing to do $U$, $x$ prevents $y$ from doing $V$; $x$ has more claim to omit doing $U$ than $y$ does have to do $V$. (UM) Now $x$ *offers* $y$ to do $U$. Then (CR) for a certain interval, $x$ is obligated to do $U$, if $y$ does $V$ within this interval (which means that $y$ *ranks before $x$*); and $x$ comes to share more responsibility than before for the consequences of $y$'s doing $V$.

($\gamma$) (PC) $x$ has offered $y$ to do $U$.[74] (UM) Now $y$ *accepts $x$'s offer* (within the crucial interval). Then (CR) $x$ is obligated to do $U$; $y$ is obligated to do $V$ (thus $y$ *is due before $x$*); and $y$ comes to share more responsibility than before for the consequences of $x$'s doing $U$.

($\delta$) (PC) By failing to do $U$, $x$ prevents $y$ from doing $V$. $y$ has requested $x$ to do $U$. (UM) Now $x$ *grants $y$'s request* to do $U$. Then (CR) $x$ has to do $U$; $y$ has to do $V$ (i.e. $y$ *is due before $x$*); and $x$ comes to share more responsibility than before for the consequences of $V$.

($\epsilon$) (PC) By failing to do $U$, $x$ prevents $y$ from doing $V$. $y$ has requested $x$ to do $U$. (UM) Now $x$ *turns down $y$'s request* to do $V$. Then (CR) $x$ has to omit $U$ (i.e. $x$ *is due before $y$*); $y$ is no more permitted to do $V$ than he was before his request; and $x$ comes to share more responsibility than before for the consequences of $V$ being left undone.

To sum up, the exceptions to the anti—collision norms could possibly be explained, with 'stepping back' for 'U' and 'driving on' for 'V', as due to the above conventional results: $x$ *is due before $y$* according to ($\alpha$), if $x$ has insisted on not stepping back, and according to ($\epsilon$), if $y$ has requested $x$ to step back and $x$ has turned down the request; $y$ *ranks before $x$* according to ($\beta$), if $x$ has offered $y$ to step back; $y$ *is due before $x$* according to ($\delta$), if $y$ has requested $x$ to step back and $x$ has granted the request, and according to ($\gamma$), if $x$ has offered $y$ to step back and $y$ has accepted the offer. — Up until now, the interpretation is mere guesswork. Its value depends on our finding suitable utterances and on

---

73) '$U$' and '$V$' are variables for behavior of $x$ and $y$, respectively.
74) This precondition serves also to determine $V$.

establishing rules according to which the utterances have the required meanings. If we take step 2, we know just what to look for; its advantage consists precisely in this heuristic help.

*Step 3*: In all cases of exception, we can discover bits of behavior and kinds of circumstances, such that to a given *kind of behavior* in given *circumstances* there can be attributed one and only one utterance meaning with the required conventional result. This implies also (1) that in each case the behavior is performed by that driver whom we assume to be the speaker because of his role in the conventional result, (2) that his behavior is perceptible for the presumed addressee, and (3) that the circumstances are public. The *kind of behavior* turns out to be the same for all situations, viz. horn honking or headlight flashing[75] (which one does not matter); we call this 'signalling'. The *circumstances* are of just two kinds: the signalling driver slows down or remains stationary on the one hand, and he speeds up or maintains his speed on the other; we call them 'hesitating' and 'pushing', respectively. The hypothetical pairing with utterance meanings is as follows (remember that in all situations, $x$ ranks before $y$):[76]

(1'')  $x$ ranks before $y$, $x$ signals; $x$ pushes: $x$ *insists* to $y$ on not stepping back.

(2'')  $x$ ranks before $y$; $x$ signals; $x$ hesitates: $x$ *offers* to $y$ to step back.

(3'')  $x$ ranks before $y$, $x$ has offered $y$ to step back; $y$ signals; $y$ pushes: $y$ *accepts $x$'s offer* to step back.

(5'')[77]  $x$ ranks before $y$, $y$ signals: $y$ *requests* $x$ to step back.

(6'')  $x$ ranks before $y$, $y$ has requested $x$ to step back; $x$ signals; $x$ pushes: $x$ *turns down $y$'s request* to step back.

(7'')  $x$ ranks before $y$, $y$ has requested $x$ to step back: $x$ signals; $x$ hesitates: $x$ *grants $y$'s request* to step back.

So far, these *utterance meaning rules* are postulated only on account of their explanatory value (via the conventional results) for the exceptions from the background conventions, and horn honking and headlight flashing are called signalling only because utterance meanings can successfully be attributed to them. Assuming these utterance meaning

---

75) This limits the present chapter to a part of the case study, viz. a fragment of NIVEAU which I call NIVEAU zero. A description which covers more signs of the signalling system has to involve sentence meaning attributions which are the topic of chapters VI and VII.

76) (1'') is a provisional version of an intermediary (1') which will eventually lead up to the final version (1). Now each rule of NIVEAU zero has a clearly identifiable substitute in NIVEAU. This is indicated by giving both the same numeral.

77) (4'') will be added later.

rules is more than mere guesswork: They help us to make sense of otherwise unexplained constant conjunctions of odd behavior, specific circumstances, and deviant conventional situations.

§ 19 Background conventions and suspected signals

In actual empirical work, success achieved so far will depend on finding an optimal balance between two elements: *choice of background conventions* should, ideally, leave us with a set of deviant situations where behavior is present which has the characteristic oddity of signalling behavior. (The relevant circumstances will be present because otherwise the situation could not be conventionally deviant; and interpreting the conventional deviation as due to an utterance meaning is just a question of creativity.) I shall not attempt to state criteria for background conventions or for signalling behavior which are generally applicable. Rather, I sum up what was helpful in recognizing both in the course of my case study.

For background conventions, the example is particularly easy. Most of the anti − collision norms are explicitly learned in driving schools, usually before meanings of using horn or headlight flash are first met with. Thus there is some probability that (BC 1) to (BC 8) are rather deeply engrained, and that in reacting to deviations drivers would tend to come up with supplementary rules rather than lose their general readiness to react according to (BC 1) to (BC 8). Furthermore, drivers regularly get into situations as those described in (BC 1) to (BC 8), and in these cases the conventional result usually holds until the encounter has passed. Again, this fact tends to reinforce a proneness to act according to (BC 1) to (BC 8) in the first place and to be aware of modifying circumstances only by way of being aware of the circumstances relevant for (BC 1) to (BC 8). In the third place, in cases where drivers get into situations described in (BC 1) to (BC 8), involvement would usually have been unavoidable. Though resulting from two intentional maneuvers, the situation is unforseeable for both drivers; there is nothing they can do about it as long as they carry out their plan to drive somewhere. Such situations are something which drivers have to take into account, just as is the case with natural events which force themselves upon them. In contrast, the modifying circumstances that we isolate as utterances only have half of this character. A driver who signals need not do so: he will react to another driver's signalling as something that need not have occurred. So he will learn to treat two kinds of conventionally relevant circumstances apart, according to whether they come like uncontrollable events that determine what he has to do or like tools that he or the other party uses to modify a situation in which they find themselves.

All this stuff is, of course, amateur psychology. If it is correct in outline, then the dispositions for reacting to (BC 1) to (BC 8) circumstances are much more deeply anchored than those for reacting to circumstances which are relevant for utterance meanings. Thus there is a certain plausibility that we should describe the whole system as consisting of two parts, viz. background conventions and utterance meaning rules, because changes in one will occur relatively independently of changes in the other. And since in a search for background conventions we can tentatively rely on considerations such as those mentioned above, there really is some prospect of isolating these conventions when preparing to describe the language (if any) that is supposed to be grafted upon them.

For some cases, a study of the function of the conventional system may help us further. Again my example is terribly easy. Compared to rituals deciphered by anthropologists, or to the rather astonishing explanations for certain kinds of social behavior in our society given to us by sociologists, the function of (BC 1) to (BC 8) for the survival of a car driving group and, thus, for the conventions' own empirical validity is abundantly clear. These conventions make up a self−contained whole in which each part must be present, unless it has a substitute; were any one part missing, the attained degree of security would abruptly decrease to a large extent. By contrast, an implementation of the signalling conventions gradually improves the system. Improvement depends on how rich the signalling conventions are and how often they are used.

Turning now to the other scale, we may tentatively list some features which make a behavior more likely to count as a case of signalling:

(1) The behavior should be easily producible. Compared with speaking, digging a ditch is hard.

(2) The behavior should be easily perceptible. Therefore, whispering would be a less likely candidate than speaking.

(3) Whether or not the addressee perceives the signalling should depend as little as possible on his attentiveness. If group members can close their ears but always keep their eyes open, then visually perceptible behavior is more suitable than acoustically perceptible behavior; the opposite holds for humans.

(4) Behavior which is to be counted as signalling should have as few other functions as possible. Eating, for example, is a bad candidate, as is singing in human behavior.

(5) Signalling behavior should be inexpensive (expenses which arise from the conventional result do not count). Setting one's house on fire is easy, and it is easily perceptible; but we should hesitate to count it as an utterance with a conventional meaning.

(6) Ways of signalling which are interchangeable without a change in utterance meaning should be kept to a minimum. The plausibility of this demand is best seen in a language in which all signs are interchangeable. The more different ways there are of signalling, the more difficult it becomes to learn them, the greater the risk of signalling inadvertently, and the greater the chance of mistaking something as signalling behavior.

These tentative remarks will not serve to classify isolated kinds of behavior either as signalling or as non—signalling behavior. They can only be used in comparing the relative merits of descriptions which make different assumptions about what counts as signalling in the group. Now flashing one's beams and honking one's horn are both easily producible and perceptible. We presently know of no other function they have for driving or elsewhere; moreover both are very cheap (reloading the battery to replace the energy consumed for flashing one's beams or honking one's horn costs next to no gasoline). Hearing a honking horn is not dependent on attention; and a flashing beam is used only if directed at the presumptive addressee's car, in which case the driver cannot help but notice it, either directly or in his rearview mirror. (Drivers' eyes are open.) And anticipating later results, we can state here that no further signals are interchangeable with honking one's horn and flashing one's headlights.

That our example is easy does not mean that it is without problems; for instance, I experimented some time with treating "pushing" and "stepping back" as ways of signalling ('intention movements', as ethologists call them). Demonstrating the case study is, however, intended to show how things work if all goes well. So let us go ahead.

## § 20 Strengthening the description

*Step 4*: When pushing is relevant for the utterance meaning, in two out of three cases hesitating is relevant too: where signalling while pushing means insisting with (1''), hesitating means offering with (2''), and where pushing means turning down a request with (6''), hesitating means granting it with (7''). However, where pushing means accepting an offer with (3''), nothing so far is said by signalling while hesitating in the same situation. There is a lacuna in our system — it lacks symmetry. We can make it more coherent if we fill in the gap between (3'') and (5'') by using our system heuristically, i.e. without being forced to do so:

(4'')   $x$ ranks before $y$, $x$ has offered $y$ to step back; $y$ signals; $y$ hesitates: *y declines x's offer* to step back.

Declining an offer can be partially explicated:

($5'$)   (PC) $x$ has offered $y$ to do $U$. (UM) Now *y declines x's offer* (within the crucial interval). Then (CR) $x$ is permitted to omit $U$; $y$ is obligated to omit $V$; and $y$ comes to share more responsibility than before for the consequences of $x$'s omitting $U$.

The conventional result implies that $x$ ranks before $y$. This is why we could not possibly notice such cases in our business of explaining exceptions to the anti−collision norms. What we have to look for, instead, are signallings−while−hesitating which are duplicated by the second party, without any conventional deviation arising. Such cases we find. We have got a deeper understanding of an apparent non−exception where in reality two successive conventional shifts took place − first to $y$'s ranking before $x$ because of $x$'s offer, then back to $x$'s ranking before $y$ because of $y$'s declining the offer. (4'') makes sense of the fact that events which are otherwise relevant for the conventional make−up sometimes cease to be so.

*Step 5*: Requesting, in (6'') and (7''), has less direct explanatory value than the remaining utterance meanings because it is only used as a pre−requisite for granting and turning down, without any operative conventional result of its own. This is found to be different within the fields of three further background conventions:

(BC 9)   The easier it is for $x$ to avoid impeding or endangering $y$ and the more $y$ would be impeded or endangered, the less $x$ is per- mitted to impede or endanger $y$.

(BC 10)   Everyone is individually responsible for the consequences of his driving maneuvers insofar as these maneuvers are not imposed upon him by law or by the maneuvers of other drivers.

(BC 11)   In which manner and direction someone drives is his own busi- ness, as long as it is not forbidden or prescribed by the Road Traffic Regulations.

Now consider the following situation: In approaching $x$ from the opposite direction, $y$ does not move to the far right, although a parked car is in $x$'s lane. If $y$ would keep well to the right, $x$ could pass the parked car at the very moment when $y$ passes it in the opposite direction. According to (BC 9), $y$ is minimally obligated to keep to the far right − minimally, because it is not that easy and because $x$ can spend one or two seconds after all. If, however, $y$ decides to keep to the far right, thereby touching the curbstone, skidding, and damaging his own or someone else's car, he alone is responsible for the damages according to (BC 10). And if $y$ keeps to the far right without any ensuing catastrophe, (BC 11) permits $x$ to slow down all the same rather than to seize the opportunity.

But now let $x$ signal while both are still approaching the critical defile; then the conventional make–up of the situation changes: $y$'s minimal obligation to move to the far right increases; if $y$ moves to the far right, $x$ shares in responsibility for ensuing damages; and if $y$ moves to the far right (without ensuing accident), $x$ is obligated to pass the parked car briskly. (None of these consequences is a legal one!) These conventional shifts could possibly be interpreted as due to $x$'s requesting $y$ to keep well to the right if the following partial explication is adopted:

($\eta$)  (PC) By failing to do $V$, $y$ prevents $x$ from doing $U$. (UM) Now $x$ *requests* $y$ to do $V$. Then (CR) $y$ becomes more obligated to do $V$; if $y$ does $V$, $x$ then will share more responsibility than before for the consequences of $V$; and if $y$ does $V$, then $x$ becomes considerably more obligated than before to do $U$.

In order to get this conventional result operating, we have to attribute to $x$'s signalling the utterance meaning that $x$ requests $y$ to keep to the far right. What further circumstances should we take as relevant for this meaning? In the variety of situations like the one above (note that in interpreting "situations like the one above", we are guided by the very precondition of ($\eta$)!) where the same deviations from (BC 9), (BC 10), and (BC 11) occur upon $x$'s signalling, we do not find any further circumstances to be necessary for the deviations to occur. Thus we try the following utterance meaning rule:

(5')  By failing to do $V$, $y$ prevents $x$ from doing $U$; $x$ signals: $x$ *requests* $y$ to do $V$.[78]

With ($\eta$), (5'') yields the conventional deviations from (BC 9), (BC 10), and (BC 11). Thus postulating an utterance meaning, which looked far–fetched as long as judged by its effects in a limited field, proves to be very fruitful if the theory is used in another area. It is, in fact, the very same theoretical entity which operates in both areas; for (5') is a strengthened version of (5''). The latter's '$x$ ranks before $y$' has been replaced by the precondition of ($\eta$).

---

78) There are two tacit restrictions to this as well as to all rules. (1) Reference is only to what $x$ and $y$ can do for the sake of driving quickly and/or safely; e.g. $x$ does not request $y$ to invite him to his birthday party. (2) The rules refer only to standard interests; e.g. $x$ does not request $y$ to give him his big Plymouth. The details of this are of interest only for the special case study.

*Step 6*: Our last observation suggests a parallel replacement, in the other utterance meaning rules, of '*x* ranks before *y*' with the preconditions of the respective explications of utterance meanings. Thus, for instance, '*x* ranks before *y*' in

(1'')    x *ranks before* y; *x* signals; *x* pushes: *x* insists to *y* on not stepping back

is replaced by the (*a*) precondition, and (1'') becomes

(1')    *By failing to do U, x prevents y from doing V. x is more entitled to omit doing U than y is to do V*; *x* signals; *x* pushes: *x* insists to *y* on omitting *U*.

It would be no good strengthening the utterance meaning rules still further by inserting conditions weaker than these preconditions − at least as long as the scope of the explications of utterance meanings is not widened by weakening their preconditions. For these must be satisfied if the explications are to yield the conventional results. On the other hand, strengthening an utterance meaning rule to this extent may turn out to be too bold. For this leaves us with hesitating and pushing as the only meaning determining elements which are specific for the language under consideration; this may be going too far. ((5') is, in fact, non−idiomatic to a surprising degree!) However, luck is on our side. Besides some minor corrections to be noted in the next section, all predictions of conventional situations due to the strengthened versions of the utterance meaning rules come out true. This is an advantage of our approach. For even if only suggested rather than required by it, the reinforcement is in line with its central idea.

## § 21 The meaning of circumstances

*Step 7*: 'Hesitating', which was short for 'slowing down or remaining stationary', and 'pushing' for 'speeding up or keeping speed' are the last remaining elements which look a bit accidental. If car drivers react to such circumstances, then perhaps they do so because these circumstances are instances of something which it is natural to react to for a driver in *such situations*. Now 'such situations' are situations as described by the preconditions of the utterance meaning explications; hesitating, in such a situation, is suitable, pushing unsuitable for the other party's interest. We could try to replace '*x* hesitates' ('pushes') by '*x* does something which is (un)suitable for *V*'. The conventional effects to be predicted will now be different in some cases; if the predictions come out true, we can hope to have found out *why* hesitating and pushing are relevant. Our rules now look like this (the italicized clause replacing 'pushes'):

(1) By failing to do *U*, *x* prevents *y* from doing *V*; *x* is more entitled to omit doing *U* than *y* is to do *V*. *x* signals and *does something which is unsuitable for y's doing V*. Thereby, *x* insists to *y* on his omitting *U*.

Our hope to have grasped the point of hesitating and pushing proves itself to be justified. On the one hand, the revised rules cover new cases where they lead to correct predictions of conventional effects. For instance, if in the narrow defile case discussed in step 5, the unimpeded driver, *y*, signals first and keeps to the far right well before reaching the defile, this is an offer only according to the final version of rule (2), because *y*'s keeping to the far right is suitable for *x*'s passing the defile at the same time as *y*. On the other hand, we can correct erroneous predictions which we have tolerated up until now. For instance, *x* may turn down *y*'s request to let him slip out into the passing lane by signalling and slowing down (contrary to the old version) if he thereby continues to block the passing lane for *y* who is stuck in behind a truck which is slowing down. This achievement counts in favor of our approach for the same reason as did the result of step 6: It is the explications of utterance meanings that suggested the improvement.

It might be instructive to add a remark on what we have actually done in taking step 7: We have, in fact, attributed meanings to circumstances. Just as it does not matter which one of two sentences we use on a given occasion, as long as both of them mean that it is going to rain, it does not matter either which one of two actions we perform on a given occasion, as long as both of them are unsuitable for what the addressee is interested in. The meaning of both sentences is what matters about them for what one can say in using them, given accompanying circumstances; being unsuitable for the addressee's interest is what matters about the actions for what one can say if they are among the circumstances which accompany one's use of a signal. I shall return to this parallel in § 42.

## § 22 Theoretical fruitfulness

*Step 8*: In explaining deviations from background conventions, up until now we have restricted our business to deviations which we stumbled upon. However, our way of explaining these facts commits us *to predict the complete conventional results* in addition to the ones we are interested in. For instance, in invoking offering as an explanation of why *y* ranks before *x* rather than vice versa, we cannot content ourselves with happily finding out that *x* really has to step back because of his offer; we also have to check whether or not this conventional make−up vanishes after a certain lapse of time unless *y* takes advantage of it. Furthermore, we have *to predict effects* according to the whole body of the conventional results *for situations due to any further background conventions*, as long as the utterance meaning rules apply to the background conventional situations. This fact of being committed to unforeseen or even new consequences — for the system of background conventions may grow — characterizes our description as an open, or theoretically fruitful, one. The longer our predictions come out right, the better we are entitled to claim that our meaning attributions are correct.

*Step 9*: The system of background conventions (BC 1) − (BC 8) could have been enlarged in such a way that those circumstances which the deviations follow upon are given a natural role; this role would be non−linguistic, however, in that neither pushing, hesitating, nor headlight flashing or horn honking are attributed utterance meanings:

(BC\*) Where *y* cannot act unless he knows how *x* will act, *x* by saliently beginning to perform a relevant action is obligated to perform it completely.

(BC\*\*) By making himself salient in a situation where he cannot act un-less he knows how *x* will act, *y* is obligated to avail himself of any opportunity created by subsequent salient behavior of *x*.

Adding (BC\*) and (BC\*\*) to (BC 1) − (BC 8) spirits away those deviations which we dealt with by the utterance meaning rules (1'') to (7''); for hesitating or pushing while either flashing or horn honking constitute the relevant bits of salient behavior. There is indeed a natural way of coming by (BC\*) and (BC\*\*) without assuming utterance meanings: People save time if in situations where they have to *wait* for others they may act upon *beginnings*, and they spare themselves errors if they are permitted to act upon *salient beginnings* only; thus the conven-tions would have a point. Since (BC\*) and (BC\*\*) are perfectly natural and enormously simpler than seven utterance meaning rules, the conventional language use hypothesis faces serious competition in the field of (BC 1) to (BC 8).

On the other hand, (BC\*) and (BC\*\*) do not suggest additional background conventions in order to cope with the obligations which we explain as imposed by requests, or with what we construe as conventional consequences of insisting, offering and so on *other than those* that were used for explaining the deviations from (BC 1) to (BC 8). Finding additional background conventions would of course be possible. But as long as there is no theoretical idea in the offing, this possibility is no more than trivial; for as Hempel's argument about the theoretician's dilemma shows,[79] what any one theory explains can be explained without it as long as we can use it to find some weaker substitute. There would scarcely be any real theory which explains why what we construe as the conventional results of utterances with given meanings always come in characteristic bundles − except a theory which postulates exactly these utterance meanings. (This consideration will bear more weight the more diverse utterance meanings come to enter into the description as its scope is enlarged.)

Note that this is not to deny that the evolution of a conventional language in which there are requests can be explained and that such an explanation has to assume a pre−linguistic stage. (I do indeed think that the sequence 'beginning to act − saliently beginning to act − sinalling while beginning to act', as a means of transporting conventional results from actions to utterances through historical time, is as good a speculation as any other on language evolution.) However, what develops out of this prelingustic stage has to be described as a language if it actually is one. If so, then such a description will be theoretically more fruitful than its language use waiving rivals. For NIVEAU zero, the complete description is given in Appendix I; it is hoped that the present chapter succeeded in establishing that such descriptions can be assessed in a methodically disciplined way. This is what counts for the philosophy of language.

---

79) "If the terms and principles of a theory serve their purpose they are unnecessary ...; and if they do not serve their purpose they are surely unnecessary. ... Hence, the terms and principles of any theory are unnecessary." Hempel, 'The Theoretician's Dilemma', p. 186.

# Chapter IV
# Conventional utterance meaning

§ 23 Language use: Conventional behavior calling for a special kind of description

Let us try to sum up what our case study has taught us about the content of the assumption that a group uses a conventional language.

Some or all of the social situations which occur in the group under consideration have conventional make − ups. From the point of view of their best description, every occurrence of a conventional make − up is covered by one of two kinds of convention: if covered by a background convention it is called a *background conventional make − up* and the situation where it occurs is called a *background conventional situation*; if not covered by a background convention, it is called a *deviant conventional make − up* and the situation where it occurs is called an *utterance situation*. Every utterance situation is an enriched background conventional situation; in a strict sense, explicit descriptions of background conventional situations therefore have to exclude those features which would turn them into utterance situations.

Every deviant conventional make − up can be construed as the effect of applying, to some background conventional make − up, the *conventional result* of an utterance which will have this result if under a certain *precondition* it has a given *utterance meaning*; from the point of view of the utterance, the deviant conventional make − up is also called the utterance's *conventional consequences*. The presence of conventions which connect utterance situations with such conventional consequences highlights the fact that the conventional system, as a whole, is impregnated with language use. In any given case, the fact that the precondition which is required for the conventional result to occur actually obtains is secured, either by the underlying background conventional situation, or by the addition of some or all of the features which have turned the background conventional situation into an utterance situation.

Background conventional situations are regarded as standard, normal cases; deviant conventional make − ups in utterance situations are regarded as wanting explanation. Since the utterance situation satisfies the precondition for an utterance with a given meaning to have a conventional result, which in turn would effect the shift from the background conventional make − up to the deviant one, there is but one fact missing for the explanation: the fact that the utterance situation is such that an utterance with the required meaning has been made.

Now the facts about the utterance situation are sufficient for the occurrence of the deviant conventional make – up. Therefore, the missing explanatory hypothesis has to both specify an element, present in the utterance situation, and to state that it is an utterance which, given some of the other features present in the utterance situation, has the required utterance meaning. There is no more warrant for this hypothesis than its explanatory value; the only possible evidence for some bit of behavior being an utterance and having a certain meaning is that this assumption helps to explain otherwise unexplainable conventional facts.

Hypotheses of this kind are *utterance meaning rules*; bodies of them make up languages. Assuming that a group uses a given conventional language is thus tantamount to assuming that the corresponding body of hypotheses is indispensable for the best description of the group's conventions.

## § 24 Conventional utterance meaning defined

Thus utterance meanings are theoretical entities which must be attributed to certain actions (which are thereby assumed to be utterances) in order to account, within a conventional system, for deviations from background conventions which are to be regarded as fundamental in this conventional system. That utterance meanings 'must be attributed' can mean two things. And I shall accordingly state two definitions: Either we postulate that it is necessary to describe the conventional system in this way; i.e. describing the conventional system as consisting of particular background conventions and of rules which assign particular meanings to certain utterances is the best (and therefore unavoidable) description. On the other hand, we can take certain background conventions for granted and let the utterance meaning rules deal with those conventional situations which deviate from the chosen background conventions. In this case, we are not requiring the resulting description to be the best one. Instead, we are requiring: first, that it is complete and correct with regard to all conventional situations (a condition which is implicit in the first alternative); second, that the rules specifiying utterance meanings are the best supplement to the background conventions.

In both cases, we must assume knowledge $\Lambda$ about the conventional results of utterances with given meanings, as exemplified in $(a)$ to $(\eta)$ above, and by the utterance meaning explications added to them in Appendix I. For me this knowledge has a different status than that of our knowledge about discovered conventions or postulated rules for utterance meanings. (Modifying $\Lambda$ would obscure the question whether the

conventional system is a language as we understand language — see §
27.) Because of this, I shall treat $\Lambda$ as constant, although I will flag the
concept of utterance meaning as 'utterance meaning $\Lambda$' to remind the
reader of the fact that opinions as to what $\Lambda$ should comprise may differ,
and that this might affect special applications of the definition.

Let $C$ be the conventional system of a group which determines for
any conventional make−up when it occurs; let $\Gamma$ specify certain
actions of group members as signallings;[80] let $BC$ comprise the
background conventions which determine those conventional
make−ups of situations in which there is no signalling according to
$\Gamma$; for signallings $\sigma$ in some situations $s$, let $\Gamma$ define $\Gamma$ $(\sigma, s)$; let $\Lambda$
define how, under certain preconditions, signallings with certain
utterance meanings change the conventional make−up of a situation.
Then

(Def. 1) the utterance meaning $\Lambda$ in $C$ of signalling $\sigma$ in $s$ is *um* iff

(1) $BC$, $\Gamma$, $\Lambda$ is the best description of $C$, and

(2) $\Gamma$ $(\sigma, {\scriptscriptstyle \curlyvee} s) = um$.

(Def. 2) the utterance meaning $\Lambda$ in $C$ relative to $BC$ of signalling $\sigma$ in
$s$ is *um* iff

(1) $BC$, $\Gamma$, $\Lambda$ is an empirically correct and complete description of $C$
and better than any $BC$, $\Gamma'$, $\Lambda$ $(\Gamma \neq \Gamma')$, and

(2) $\Gamma$ $(\sigma, s) = um$.

In our case study, $BC$ comprises (BC 1) to (BC 11), $\Gamma$ comprises (1) to
(7) and $\Lambda$ comprises ($a$) to ($\eta$); added to these are the supplements in
Appendix I. We may imagine $\Lambda$ as comprising everything we know about
the conventional results of any utterance meanings whatsoever; $\Lambda$ will
then be constant for different languages, which are embedded in different
conventional systems $C$.

The definition is framed to apply to languages which do not distinguish between different ways of signalling, i.e. where using different
means of signalling makes no difference in the utterance meaning, as is
the case with NIVEAU zero. All rules of NIVEAU zero are of the form
'If the situation $s$ is of kind $R$, and if $x$ signals in $s$, then his signalling
means *um*'. Therefore relevant differences between ways of signalling
might be incorporated in the specification of $R$ ('if the situation is such
that the specific sign $\sigma$ is used', or something like this); but I shall
postpone this until I have stated a definition of sentence meaning in § 40.
Both of the above definitions are a bit careless in that variables for

---

80) In the definition, I stick to this term in place of 'utterance' in order to avoid
unwarranted connotations.

speaker and addressee do not show up explicitly; hopefully the case study has made it sufficiently clear how they enter into the picture.

Ascribing conventional utterance meanings to actions is as good as this provides a good theory of the group's conventional behavior. If we want to know whether a given action by a member of a group has a conventional utterance meaning, then we have to look for the best theory of the group's conventional behavior. We have to answer our question in accordance with this theory. If, according to the best theory, the action has a conventional utterance meaning, then it is an utterance and the agent spoke in performing it. (The best theory may not exist. In this case, some utterances may lack utterance meanings in an absolute sense.)

Of course, we shall never know in an epistemologically ambitious sense whether or not the best theory which we can find actually is the best theory. Thus the ontological statement has its epistemological corrolary: We have to answer our question in accordance with the best theory which we can find. If, according to this theory, the action has a conventional utterance meaning, then we have to assume that it is an utterance and that the agent spoke in performing it. If applied to the members of the linguistic community themselves, this sounds funny: A speaker does not know, in an epistemologically ambitious sense, if he spoke, and if so, what he said; nor do addressee and audience, even if understanding him, know what he said in an epistemologically ambitious sense. [81)]

The funny sound results from two possible misinterpretations of the epistemologically ambitious sense of 'know': Speaker and addressee do know what has been said in the sense of knowing how; furthermore, they do know it in a down−to−earth sense of knowing that.

They generally know it in the sense of knowing how because, in general, they are prepared for the utterance's conventional result; lest they were so, the conventional result would not obtain. That is, they know how to deal with the utterance. Therefore, unless they knew, in this sense, what has been said, nothing would have been said at all. A speaker who generally does not know, in this sense, what he says is no competent speaker at all.

More than that, there is a justified presumption that speakers as well as addressees and audiences know what has been said even in a down−to−earth sense of knowing that. If someone learns a language, he acquires the capacity to say the same things as other speakers do, and to

---

81) Rosemarie Rheinwald suggested that this might be taken as evidence against the present approach.

decide whether he (or somebody else) said the same thing as any speaker. Such decisions are put to test in numerous ways in actual communication (just recall a witness giving evidence on what somebody said), and there can hardly be any doubt that any translation, into observers' language, of 'He said that ...' will have to handle such utterances with the principle of charity in mind. Therefore, expressions of such opinions have more than a fair chance to come out correct under any translation.

## § 25 Neptune: Conventional perturbations and their best explanation

All this seems downright complicated, at least as complicated as Gricean intentions on, say Strawson level. And perhaps some readers may raise their eyebrows, claiming this to be a dirty trick, especially invented to overcome obvious difficulties of a decidedly anti—intentionalist approach to meaning. On the pretext of such possible misgivings, I will recall an often—used story from the history of astronomy. Readers who become bored with comparisons between third—hand[82] astronomy and philosophy of language are kindly asked to ignore this section.

Since 1781, Uranus was considered to be the outermost planet of the solar system. (Observed previously, it was only in 1781 that Herschel discovered Uranus to be a planet.) Enough observations of Uranus had been made to determine how the laws of planetary motion could be applied to it; something like, but more sophisticated than Kepler's laws. In this manner a formula could be determined for representing Uranus' orbit around the sun. I have never seen this formula and would probably have difficulties understanding it. For our purposes here I will call it the 'Uranus formula'. The Uranus formula was not just refined Kepler. Rather, as determined by Alexis Bouvard of Paris in 1820, the formula also took into account the mutual gravitational influences of Jupiter, Saturn, and Uranus with the help of Pierre Laplace's *Mécanique céleste*. Thus it was a rather complicated formula. What is important for my comparison is not that the formula was simple, but that it was the best description of Uranus' orbit that could be found, which went on the assumption that beyond Uranus there was no other planet travelling around the sun.

But whereas celestial mechanics worked very well in general, the Uranus formula proved unable to deal with all observational data within the admissible limits of error. There were what scientists, in their

---

82) All historical facts and all quotations are from *Encyclopedia Britannica*, 1971, s.v. "Neptune".

unshakeable epistemological optimism, are likely to call 'deviations' or 'perturbations'. The Uranus formula was not wrong at all, and the orbit determined by it was not simply not Uranus' orbit − on the contrary, Uranus failed to keep its orbit. True Popperians call such perturbations refutations; they congratulate scientists on their increase in knowledge and recommend thinking up alternative theories. To their despair, the scientists politely refuse congratulation and plot ancillary hypotheses as soon as all true Popperians are out of sight. Since the orbit determined by the Uranus formula was as decent, consistent, and comfortable an orbit for a planet as one could wish for, there plainly must have been something which somehow seduced Uranus to leave it. The idea that the deviations were due to the influence of some planet travelling beyond Uranus came to several astronomers before 1840. The actual orbit would then be the result of two components − the proper orbit itself and the diversion due to unknown planets.

For the layman it is fascinating to learn that for two excellent mathematicians the available observations could have been sufficient for predicting future positions of the suspected planet going on the assumption that one planet was responsible for Uranus' deviation from its proper orbit. In 1845, solutions were found independently by both U.J.J. Leverrier and J.C. Adams. The results of these two astronomers coincided closely with each other. This encouraged comparison of the relevant region with star charts at the Berlin Observatory, and "it was found that an eighth magnitude star now visible was not on the chart. On the following evening the object was again looked for and found to have moved. The existence of the planet was thus established." There, then, was Neptune.

The point of the comparison is that Adam's and Leverrier's calculations represent inferences to the best explanation of perturbations in what would otherwise be a sound system. Going on the assumption that Uranus was the outermost planet in the solar system, the Uranus formula was the best description which could be found for its motion. It corresponds to our background conventions which are the best we can find for conventional behavior if we go on the assumption that the group members do not use a conventional language. Both systems manifest perturbations: Uranus deviated from the expected orbit; the conventional make−up of some situations deviates from the expected make−up. Adams and Leverrier argued in the following way: If the deviations are due to the influence of one planet travelling beyond Uranus, then this planet must have a certain orbit. It follows from the nature of this orbit that the planet will be visible at such and such a position in September 1846. For their argument, they relied on the astronomical knowledge available to them. In the same way, we have argued the following: If the shift from 'x ranks before y' to 'x is due before y' (see § 18) is in a given case due to somebody's having insisted on his priority then it must be true that anybody signalling in certain circumstances thereby insists on his priority and that the relevant person has signalled under appropriate circumstances in the given case. For this inference, we relied on our knowledge of what it is to insist on one's priority.

The comparison is lacking in one important respect: Whereas we can discover that a heavenly body is a planet without knowing whether it exerts influence on other bodies, we cannot know that an action is a meaningful utterance unless we know that it has a conventional result. (This difference disappears as soon as gravitation is taken to be something irrevocable, but I think it is only fair to agree that planets are not defined by Newton's Law of Gravitation in the way that an utterance's being meaningful is defined by its place in the network of conventions.) On the other hand, there are important similarities which underscore the comparison. At least two astronomers — Lalande in 1795, and Challis in 1846 — had observed Neptune without discovering that it was a planet: if one looks at a silvery speck in isolation one cannot determine whether it is a planet. In the same way, one can observe utterances without recognizing that they are utterances; observing a behavioral pattern in isolation is useless for determining whether it is an utterance. Second, assuming that an undetected planet exerts influence on a known planet commits one to the assumption that it exerts influcence on all known planets, and assuming that diversion is due to the planet means predicting acceleration; in the same way, assuming actions of a given kind to be instances of insisting commits one to the expectation that the conventional result of insisting will follow all such actions, and assuming that a conventional change is due to insisting commits one to all conventional results of insisting. Third, it is better to make one nearby planet responsible than to assume an accidental linear string of more distant heavenly bodies; likewise using just one meaning rule to account for many conventional changes makes this rule more fruitful than using two or three for the same purpose. And last but not least: If Neptune had not been found, astronomy would have had to look for different explanations; if we fail to discover a suitable meaning — rule then we cannot use the conventional perturbations to argue for the existence of a language.

## § 26 Expressions and expressive power

Our definition of utterance meaning, as applied to NIVEAU zero, is sufficient to prove wrong one important assumption about how things can be said. It seems to be implicitly presupposed in much current philosophy of language insofar as this deals with the meanings of utterances instead of restricting itself to sentences. Although it is difficult to find explicit statements of the assumption, on the other hand it is hard to see how some common ways of asking questions and treating problems could be accepted unless it were endorsed. The assumption says that

> the crucial disadvantage of a language which does not permit the formation of new sentences is that it cannot be used to say new things.

Apparently, this is the reason why recursive syntax is nowadays almost treated as a necessary condition for a natural language − or at any rate for an interesting one: "Any interesting language has infinitely many sentences."[83] Let us leave aside ambiguity and indexicality (for I do not have the trivial intention of proving the assumption wrong by appealing to such phenomena). The assumption then presupposes that if there is a finite stock of sentences, then there is a finite stock of things to be said, i.e. a finite number of utterance meanings. Precisely this follows from John Searle's 'principle of expressibility':

> "...for any meaning $X$ and any speaker $S$ whenever $S$ means (intends to convey, wishes to communicate in an utterance, etc.) $X$ then it is possible that there is some expression $E$ such that $E$ is an exact expression of our formulation of $X$."[84]

If this is to mean a fortiori[85] that for anything a speaker can say (not only mean), i.e. for any conventional utterance meaning, there is at least one most explicit or sufficiently explicit sentence to be used to say it, and if for two different utterance meanings such explicit sentences have to be different (since otherwise they wouldn't be sufficiently explicit), then there can be at most as many utterance meanings as there are explicit sentences presumably expressing just those utterance meanings.[86]

---

83) D. Lewis, *Convention*, p. 165.

84) *Speech Acts*, p. 20.

85) "a fortiori", because what can be said can be meant.

86) Searle's cautious qualification "it is possible that there is some expression $E$" is explained *l.c.*, p. 20: "I can in principle at least enrich the language by introducing new terms or other devices into it." It is far from obvious that every language ought

My disproof of the assumption consists in presenting NIVEAU zero where this is false. As can be easily seen, although it contains only two interchangeable signs, in this fragment of NIVEAU indefinitely many utterance meanings are generated because their propositions are determined by features of the utterance situation which may be new to any participants in the situation. New technical or legal developments could, for example, lead to drivers acquiring new interests in each others' behavior; this would create new possible propositions in utterance meanings. Note that this holds true even if the illocutionary force is constant. Thus what the utterance situation contributes to what is said — over and above disambiguating and filling indexical gaps — cannot be reduced to determining the illocutionary force. (I shall return to this question in § 43.)

I cited John Searle's 'principle of expressibility' because it contains a principle which, in my opinion, uncovers the mistake behind any attempt to connect the stock of things you can say in using some language to its stock of expresions:

> Making an utterance meaning more explicit, more clear, and more well—defined consists in making the expression that is used in making the utterance more explicit.

Although there is some truth in this idea, it is wrong in principle. If we are seduced to embrace it, then this is because we are concentrating on one of two possibilities of speaking more clearly, viz. using more explicit sentences. The other possibility consists in seeing to it that the utterance situation is sufficiently specific so that some utterance meaning rule definitely applies.

It is only natural for native speakers of fully developed natural languages to prefer the first method, for in most cases it is much easier to reformulate one's sentence than to rearrange the situation. And we shouldn't be surprised when philosophers of all people forget the second

---

Continued:

to provide for self—enrichment (NIVEAU does not); and it is still less plausible that any language ought to provide for so opulent self—enrichment that every utterance meaning which can be produced, can be procuded completely independently of the utterance situation, solely by virtue of the expression which is used. — It is important to distinguish between a language's providing conventional means for introducing new terms and its ability to grow naturally; a distinction which is closely connected with that between introducing terms and teaching. See my 'Das normative Fundament der Sprache: Ja und Aber', esp. pp. 148—150, 155—158.

possibility. Philosophers are educated people, selected among other things for their profession by a process which favors an addiction to verbosity. However, we should not lose sight of people who have the gift of clarifying their request for a tool by touching the piece they are working on.

All utterance meanings in NIVEAU zero involve references to speaker and addressee in the rendering of the illocutionary force. For most of them this is also the case in the renderings of their propositions, which additionally involve at least implicit references to the time and place of the utterance. It might therefore be argued that horn and beams are somehow indexical: No wonder they can be used to express different propositions on different occasions! But indexicality is not an illuminating diagnosis for context dependence in NIVEAU zero. The point is not that for a given behavior different speakers at different times and places can use their beams in asking different addressees, according to (5), that *they* do it *here* and *now* in *their* own favor, thus making utterances whose meanings would contain different propositions on each occasion. Rather, my point is that *the thing to do* can be different in different utterance situations. I don't believe that this fact is covered by any usual concept of indexicality.

Of course, we might broaden our concept of indexicality, calling 'indexical' any expression which, without being ambiguous, can be used to make utterances whose propositions vary according to context. Then horn and beams would be indexical expressions in NIVEAU zero. However, I think we can agree that widening the concept in this way would not be very illuminating. On the contrary, it would obscure the fact that the rules specifying the context dependence of the meanings of utterances of sentences like 'I feel fine', 'London is south of *that* mountain', 'Margaret regrets *it*', or perhaps of 'Keep *left*', 'London comes *after* Reading', may be alike in ways in which the context dependence of propositions of utterance meanings in NIVEAU zero is not.

If we accept NIVEAU zero as a natural language, it would not prove that my target assumption is wrong for English and German, although the assumption is wrong for one natural language. Two points are pertinent here: On the one hand, NIVEAU zero shows that far from being trivial, our target assumption makes a substantial claim about languages like English or German. On the other hand, a lot speaks for the assumption that languages like English or German contain large fragments which are similar to NIVEAU zero in that they use features of the utterance situation in ways other than interpreting inedexicals and disambiguating.

The most salient examples for this are conventional gestures and one—word utterances. Such utterances, of course, are not focused upon by theories of meaning which concentrate primarily on assertive uses of indicative sentences.


## § 27 The diversity of language

It is not necessary that every utterance meaning which is possible in one language be possible in any other language as well. Or, to put this more modestly, that one can say exactly the same things in all languages. For instance, there seems to be no utterance meaning in German which would be precisely like the meaning of uttering 'How do you do?' if first presented to one's hostess. However, if we want to give this question a precise meaning, then we will have to specify criteria according to which utterances in different languages can have the same utterance meaning. Such criteria should at least leave one pretheoretical intuition intact: The very fact that two persons live in groups which follow two different conventional systems must not exclude the theoretical possibility of one of them making an utterance some time which has exactly the same utterance meaning as some utterance of the other. Let us imagine the first group to adhere to the convention that the good Lord created man to help his neighbor — come hell or high water — unless it is practically impossible for him. In the second group, on the other hand, nobody is expected to help anybody unless he basically has nothing better to do. In the first group, a request will be likely to obligate the addressee, whereas in the second group, it will create no such obligation. The conventional make—ups created by both utterances thus differ. This fact, taken by itself, should not exclude the possibility of the two requests being intertranslatable.

According to the above definitions of utterance meaning, it is an open question whether or not there can be the same request in both proups. There is no guarantee for this, but the mere possibility is not excluded by the fact that both groups endorse extreme forms of altruism and egotism, respectively. This is a difference in background conventions, and it is sufficient to explain why divergent conventional make—ups follow two utterances even if these have identical meanings. The divergence is due to conventional shifts which are identical in the sense of being covered by identical descriptions. Travelling the same distance in the same direction from different points takes you to different endpoints.

Of course, our specification of $\Lambda$ must be the same in our descriptions of both languages. It would be senseless to ask whether or not there can be the same request in both languages if requesting were explicated differently in both cases. At any rate, it is not very helpful to learn that two utterances in different cultures are both requests – except for the fact that requests are different speech acts in both cultures. Comparing particular languages presupposes a stable concept of language. Nontheless, the specification of $\Lambda$ is open to dispute, and disputes may go deeper than just touching marginal features. Let me first give two examples on how to modify the central properties of the speech act of thanking/apologizing and of reproaching.

In Appendix I, I interpret the conventional result of both thanking and apologizing as being equivalent to a ritual compensation for a benefit which the speaker received from the addressee and for a disadvantage which he inflicted upon him, respectively. Both speech acts might instead be construed such that the speaker's responsibility towards the addressee is underscored. In this way the addressee's claim that his achieved status one up on the speaker (a status he reached by treating the speaker well or by being harmed by him) would be acknowledged and thereby secured. Both speech acts would then make sense if combined with two background conventions, one stating that one has to be openly servile to superiors, the other on stating that treating somebody well or being harmed by him makes one his superior. The conventional result of both thanking and apologizing would consist in the speaker freeing himself from the obligation of being openly servile. If we imagine a group with such background conventions and with signallings which have such a conventional result, then the temptation to label them as thanks or apologies would be strong. In a similar way, reproaching could be characterized as a way of stigmatizing or denouncing the addressee rather than as a way of punishing him (as in Appendix I). In combination with the background convention that it is up to the person who has been harmed to ask the whole group to apply sanctions, reproaching would have the conventional result of making the addressee liable to sanctions on the part of uninvolved people, which would not be warranted on account of his behavior towards the speaker. (Rejecting a reproach might then be interpreted as a warning not to apply sanctions.)

Both examples show that even the essential nature of a speech act may be open to dispute. Another uncertainty is exemplified by the question whether or not a conventional element recurring in the alleged conventional results of many utterance meanings can truly be ascribed to these utterance meanings after all. Several of our explications of utterance meanings state that the speaker becomes more responsible for the consequences of certain actions of the addressee's. Now in all these cases, by the utterance the addressee is obligated (or is more obligated than before) to perform his action; thus instead of incorporating, within the conventional result of the utterance, the speaker's increase in responsibility, we may achieve the same effect by asssuming an additional background condition which states that when $x$ obligates $y$ to do something, $x$ thereby becomes co−responsible for the consequences.

The openness of our concept of a language − as it is defined by $\Lambda$ − can be illustrated by a thought experiment. Let us imagine the following situation: In describing the conventional behavior of some group we have come upon several rules, which assign meanings to specified ways of signalling under well−defined circumstances, relative to background conventions which appear very natural. However, a large number of behavioral patterns remains. They conform to our specifications of signalling and lead to changes in the conventional make−up of the utterance situation if they appear under circumstances which fit in well with our elaborated system of rules. Unfortunately, however, we are not successful in construing the conventional changes as due to utterance meanings. If we forget our imperfect theoretical creativity and our blindness, which could hinder us in choosing better background conventions, then it may well be the case that our concept of language is too poor to do justice to the group's (putative) language.

An extreme case of this would be a situation where we discovered a group following conventions, which could be best described by some $BC$, $\Gamma$, $\Lambda'$; where $\Lambda'$ would be like our usual $\Lambda$, except for the fact that speaker and addressee were systematically exchanged. Whenever some $x$ says something to $y$ according ro $\Lambda$, $x$ is the addressee and $y$ the speaker according to $\Lambda'$. If we substitute $\Lambda'$ for $\Lambda$, then we end up with a fine description. Members of this group do not promise; rather in making their utterance they get the addressee to promise them something. They do not inform, but get their addressee to inform them, and so on. Let us assume the following: After empirical investigation we find that − to a random degree − it is unlikely that there is a hidden mechanism, by which the person whom we would like to have as speaker gets the person whom we would like to have as addressee to signal, thus producing, in this roundabout way, a signalling which is visible to the person we would like to have as addressee. If this were the case, then we would be pretty much at a loss with our concept of what a language might look like.

## § 28 The theoretical character of the speech act of reference[87)]

The first point we can note about reference is that statements like 'In uttering $\sigma$ in $s$, the speaker referred to $a$' are high up in the theoretical stories of the description which we accept of the language the speaker is using. We reach the first story when we accept one of several descriptions which, in light of behavioral evidence, fits the bill in accounting for the group's conventions. We reach the second story by using $\Lambda$ to systematically account for certain irregularities. We get to the third story by assuming a certain language and suitable background conventions (one pair out of many ones that are still possible, given $\Lambda$). Only in the third story can utterance meanings be specified; propositons enter into the picture because $\Lambda$ binds us in most cases to specify utterance meanings as pairs of illocutionary forces and propositions. Since no one refers unless the meaning of his utterance contains a (possibly incomplete) proposition, any attribution of reference is preceded by decisions which were already made at three previous stories. Divergent decisions could readily have led to divergent reference attributions, especially when one is in agreement about such facts as the speaker's state of mind.[88)]

Therefore, to say that a person refers to something is not to give a non—committal description. Rather, we can only speak like this when we have made a number of decisions on the path which eventually led us to describe the conventional behavior of the group in question. None of the decisions are arbitrary; but neither are any forced upon us. Our decision is based on reasons of theoretical fruitfulness; and deciding differently will normally lead to diverging views about whom or what the speaker is referring to.[89)]

There is a further reason for the non—uniqueness of reference. The language we have hypothetically imputed may specify all meanings of utterances uniquely, or else it may specify some utterance meanings in different ways (equivalent with respect to the conventional result), assigning to the utterance two different pairs of illocutionary forces and propositions, as in '$x$ tells $y$ that the bull is dangerous' (where $x$ refers to

---

87) Keeping within the limits of what is established by the case study, this section is on reference as far as it can be in disregarding structural information. In particular, it is not on so—called referring expressions.

88) "If God had looked into our minds he would not have been able to see there whom we were speaking of." Wittgenstein, *Philosophical Investigations* II xi, p. 217e.

89) If we disregard the different empirical basis − *truth conditions* of *sentences* instead of *conventional consequences* of *utterances* −, the result of my case study confirms Davidson's proposal in 'Reality without reference'.

the bull rather than to the addressee) and 'x warns y not to approach the bull' (where x refers to the addressee, the proposition being that y does not approach the bull). I don't think that we would like to classify this case as one where the speaker says two things at a time, as when, in uttering 'Yes!', he both answers a question in the course of a telephone conversation as well as one asked by somebody present, thus saving one utterance. In the latter example it is somehow accidental that the utterance meaning is specifiable in two different ways, whereas in the warning case, if the language in question is as imagined, the double specifiability is non — accidental. So people who tend to assume that an utterance *achieves* to be about the world *by way of* the speaker referring to some part of that world may be satisfied in the answering example where referring to two different things at a time goes hand in hand with saying two different things at a time. However, they will be less satisfied in the warning case where the speaker seems to say just one thing but either refers to something or not, depending on how we specify what he says. Actually, there is no problem at all: Given that his language provides for two different specifications of one utterance meaning, there is no more a contradiction between 'with u, x refers to y' and 'with u, x does not refer to y' than there is between 'this building lacks a wall' and 'this building does not lack a wall'. For the building may be viewed either as a castle or as a manor house (just as the utterance may be viewed either as a warning or as a report) because our best architectural theory provides both specifications. Anyhow we will not complain that it is inscrutable whether the building lacks a wall, because we can view it either as a castle or as a manor house.

For still a third reason the reference of an utterance can appear fuzzy. This reason can be illustrated by the following example. Let us imagine two languages: Whereas in the first language, one can report that one elephant is nearby, that two elephants are nearby, and that between three and ten elephants are nearby, in the second language, one can report that one elephant is nearby, that two elephants are nearby, that three are nearby, ..., that ten elephants are nearby. In neither language is it possible to report that there are eleven or more elephants nearby; nor can one report in the second language that there are three or four or ... or ten elephants nearby. If a speaker of the second language wants to give a correct report on three to ten elephants, then it is obligatory for him to report on a definite number. On the other hand, the most specific report that a speaker of the first language can give is to report that there are between three and ten elephants nearby. Whether he is reporting that there are between three and ten or whether he is reporting something more specific depends on what the best description of his language is, i.e. which description best accounts for the conventional behavior of his group. If, according to the best description of his language, he reports on between three and ten elephants, then he is reporting neither on three nor on four nor ... nor on ten. For a speaker of the second language, this fact might seem rather puzzling, because he himself cannot utter such a report in his own language. There is something which a speaker of the second language cannot say, but which a speaker of the first language can say, though in a certain sense the second language is richer than the first.

Now imagine that some philosopher has a fairly firm view about the different types of entities a speaker might alternatively be referring (or purporting to refer) to — for example, physical objects, views of physical objects, undetached parts of physical objects, temporal states of physical objects (like water), and finally universals of which physical objects are instances. It is a fair guess that this view has been influenced by the different types of expressions and constructions which his own language (e.g. English) provides him with. E.g., because he can say 'This is the same rabbit as that', thereby definitely referring to a physical object, he is disposed to report on the utterances of others as referring to physical objects; and because he can, although dislikes to, say 'These are two different instances of one and the same rabbithood', he is disposed to report on the utterances of others as at least purporting to refer to universals; and so on. Let us now imagine our philosopher to be confronted with some language where there is no plausible description which specifies utterance meanings such that speakers are said to refer to any of the types of entities in our philosopher's repertoire. For our philospher, this will indeed be puzzling if he thinks that in order to say something meaningful speakers must refer to something. But actually there is no problem at all as can readily be seen if we imagine physical objects to be dropped from our philosopher's repertoire and if we let speakers refer precisely to them — something our philsopher could not even dream of. So his problem really consists in either devising some ingenious type of referent, new to him, which one may construe speakers to be referring to, or else renouncing his conviction that, come what may, they must refer to something. The second alternative amounts to no more than agreeing that some very specific description of conventional behavior fails.

# Chapter V
# Against intentionalism

## § 29 Preliminaries

The present chapter is devoted to an attack on intentionalist theories of conventional utterance meaning. Three *caveats* in advance. The first has to do with 'attack': Although I shall try to be methodical in distinguishing between reasons for assuming such theories to be wrong, on the one hand, and reasons for being suspicious about one's motives for taking them to be true on the other (reasons that could consist either in recognizing the falsity of reasons which supposedly confirm intentionalist theories or in diagnosing suspected confusions), I am more interested in provoking new arguments than in presenting a conclusive case. The second *caveat* concerns 'intentionalist': My target is in fact any theory (of conventional utterance meaning) which makes conventional utterance meaning dependent upon speaker's (or speakers') meaning; that is, any theory which subscribes to the view that 'meaning is where something is meant'.[90] But without being misleading, one cannot speak of 'meaning theories of meaning' (as can be nicely done in German: 'Meinenstheorien der Bedeutung'). And since all such theories on the market are intentionalist theories of speaker's meaning, I take exception in identifying my target non−analytically by using a description which is definite for empirical reasons. The third *caveat* has to do with 'conventional utterance meaning': As soon as meaning becomes regular, or conventional, or linguistic, many people tend to speak of sentence meaning. But I am confident that they will agree to the following: if not even conventional utterance meaning is tied to speaker's/s' meaning, then for sentence meaning this will be even less so.

---

90) Paradigmatic for this approach are: H.P: Grice, 'Meaning' and 'Utterer's Meaning, Sentence Meaning, and Word Meaning'; D. Lewis, *Convention*; St. Schiffer, *Meaning*; J. Bennett, *Linguistic Behaviour*; G. Meggle, *Grundbegriffe der Kommunikation*; A. Jones, *Communication and Meaning*. The strategy is intentionalist in a double way: When a speaker says something meaningful, he should in normal cases do so by way of meaning it; and linguistic conventions are to hold thanks to the community's members' intentions. Lewis was the first to try to secure the first aim by securing the second (see above, § 15). The intentionalist approach is so absolutely dominating present Anglo−Saxon philosophy of language that exceptions are met with only accidentally. The ones known to me only include, besides those mentioned in fn. 4, p. 11: J. Biro, 'Conditions for Phatic Acts: A Non−mentalistic Analysis', 'Conventionality in Speech Acts', and 'Intentionalism in the Theory of Meaning'; and D. Lumsden, 'Does Speaker's Reference Have Semantic Relevance?'

## § 30 Ignored motives for making constative utterances

In the Gricean sense,[91] a speaker means something by uttering $u$ only if he utters $u$ with a certain motive and, putting any particulars aside, this motive determines what he means. In the literature, there is a preoccupation with constative utterances where the speaker means that $p$. Here the speaker's motive is his desire that the addressee acquires the belief that $p$. I would ask the reader to consider whether there aren't motives for making constative utterances which on the whole are just as common as the desire to get the addressee to believe something and where achieving one's aim does not depend, either in fact or according to speakers' views, on getting their addressees to believe something. I don't want to contest that the desire to get the addresseee to believe something is a frequent motive for constative utterances. I simply want to question its centrality. My list is neither systematic nor is it intended to be complete; it contains items that I could not help but notice in observing everyday speech behavior.

Let us think of people who have just witnessed an accident, or who were watching fireworks, or who saw that Miss Dove, the elderly teacher, just had coffee with the handsome, young and newly arrived chaplain. These people latch on to the very next person they chance to meet to tell him about the respective accident, fireworks, or tête à tête. They have but one motive: they have had a rousing experience, they are all worked up about it and must get it out of their systems, and this they do. It is very much like saying "Ouch" if something hurts. The very same thing happens when the addressee observes something himself, noticing everything which the utterance might inform him about: "The sun is rising!" For my part, I am very impressed by this use of constative utterances for expressing experiences. Much of the talk I overhear in the street is of this kind; people often use this manner of speaking when they are not paying attention to how they are speaking and what they are saying; and it is extremely frequent among children. I confess to be biased in favor of unreflected talk as well as of children's talk when looking for the foundations of language.

---

91) See H.P. Grice, 'Meaning', 'Utterer's Meaning and Intentions', and 'Meaning Revisited'; P.F. Strawson, 'Intention and Convention in Speech Acts'; J. Searle, *Speech Acts*, ch. 2, sect. 6; St. Schiffer, *Meaning*, pp. 49–68; G. Meggle, *Grundbegriffe der Kommunikation*, Kap. 6.2. Plausible revisions have been proposed in J. Bennett, *Linguistic Behaviour*, pp. 124–133; and in A. Kemmerling, 'Was Grice mit "meinen" meint' and 'Utterer's Meaning Revisited'.

Needless to say, in such cases speakers do not care whether or not anyone believes them. And even if they did care, their reaction to trust and to doubt would manifest either thankfulness for being accepted or disappointment for being rejected, but not any cognitive reassurance or challenge. These speakers simply did not say what they said in order to convince their addressees of its truth. The same holds for my second example, viz. people who make constative utterances for the sole motive of winning attention by assuming the role of the knowing person. Think of the small child of about six or eight who has learned that people draw attention to themselves by telling stories and who tries this out for himself; or of the show – off who is listened to because his stories are as fascinating as they are unbelievable, although not intended to be fairy-tales. In both cases the speaker does not intend to get his hearers to believe what he is telling them. Although that would be fine with him, it is not his aim. Rather he enjoys being the center of attention,[92] and he can keep this position up as long as no one says: "That's a tall – tale, if I ever heard one, Henry!", or "What nonsense!", or "Come off it!".

This behavior is parasitic upon a different role – or different roles – of constative utterances, of course; but as yet there is no hint at what it might be parasitic upon. Getting hearers to believe something may be parasitic upon other uses of language too; and I shall argue this in § 32. As long as we are looking for people's motives for making constative utterances (motives which are not reached by getting hearers to believe something), attracting other people's attention is a perfectly good and very frequent motive. People try to gain attention in all ways.

A third motive is that of getting rid of responsibilities. The solicitor informs his client that in suing his opponent there is a risk of losing the case; the surgeon informs his patient about the average mortality rates of a complicated operation; the civil servant jots down a memo for the files, briefly summarizing for his superior the points of a talk the had with another official. None of the above need to be interested in convincing his addressee. If anything, the solicitor and surgeon would even be interested in leaving him unimpressed; the civil servant might share this interest because he is hostile to his superior's political outlook. But this is unimportant. What matters is that all of the speakers have one and the same motive in informing their addressee: They want to deprive him of

---

92) This interpretation is far from trivial; in accepting it, I am following a proposal from Teresa Jacobsen.

the opportunity of pleading non—knowledge, if, by ignoring the information, he subsequently runs into trouble — has to pay lawsuits, is permanently disabled, or cannot pay the costs for the air force's new fighter—bomber. Careful observation of everyday talk reveals many similar occurrences where people utter something for the sole reason of being able to say later on: "I told him so."

In view of my conception concerning which conventional result characterizes an utterance as that of a speaker who informs the addresse that $p$ — namely that the addressee may rely on $p$ at the speaker's expense —I cannot help but regard the third motive as central to the whole business of informative talk. If, in the case that I am wrong, I take responsibility for my addressee's difficulties, then he cannot claim that he simply was in no position to act as would have been appropriate if I were right. Either I am right or I pay up; and his claim not to have been in a position to act is precisely what his excuse (that he did not know) would amount to. The fourth motive I want to point out is even more closely related to my view; it occurs frequently in connection with comments on orders, like: "Would you get me the bucket, please. It's on the balcony!" In explaining that the bucket is on the balcony, the speaker is not interested in convincing the hearer of this fact; what he is interested in is that the addressee acts as if the bucket were where the speaker says it is. The addressee does not even need to believe that the speaker believes that the bucket is on the balcony, nor does the speaker need to want to convince the addressee that he himself believes this. If the speaker issues an order and explains how it is to be carried out, then it is not the addressee's business to chime in with his own opinion. What the speaker wishes is that his statement is treated as true, rather than for it to be believed or for him to be believed to be honest.

The fifth and last motive I want to draw attention to concerns cases where everybody knows that $p$ and where everybody knows that everybody knows that $p$. (The latter clause distinguishes this case from the examination example where only the candidate knows that the examiner knows that $p$, but not vice versa.) If the speaker then states that $p$, he cannot hope either to convince his addressee that $p$ is the case or that the speaker believes it to be the case. In the cases I have in mind the speaker states that $p$ in order to secure something like a common notification of $p$; his stating that $p$ commits the addressee to not questioning it in the future if failing to question it now. Examples from official contexts include the committee chairman who finds that the quorum is present or that the majority has rejected a motion. Such utterances are not explicit performatives, e.g. 'verdictives' in Austin's sense. The speaker's utterance "I find that the quorum is present" does not make the quorum present, and committee members can challenge it by pointing out that only nine of the eleven required members are present. If nobody objects and if it subsequently turns out that there is no quorum (although no one has left), then in challenging a decision it is prohibited for members to argue from this fact, precisely because they have joined the committee chairman in notifying that the quorum is present. And it is this common notification which the chairman intended.

There are plenty of less official examples. Think of two engineers who are trying to find out why a machine has broken down and who, whenever they have checked off a point in their repair's manual, finding it to be o.k., say: "Well, that one's o.k.." They thereby ensure agreement on what the trouble is not. What they desire is efficient cooperation in their continuing search for the defect, where efficiency depends on their treating the same things as well — functioning. Or think of a couple in a car who want to got to Churchvillage which — as both know — lies between two churchless villages. As they see a churchless village on the left, another churchless one on the right, and one with a church in the middle the wife says: "Look, the middle one is Churchvillage", and her husband answers: "You're right, let's go there." As far as I understand couples in cars, the dialogue has but one function: to ensure that neither can complain to the other if the village should turn out not to be Churchvillage after all. The wife neither desires to convince her husband, nor does he desire to reassure her. Both agreed on taking the consequences. That's all there is to it.

With this we have five sample motives for making constative utterances that $p$; motives where there is no desire either to convince the addressee of $p$ or to convince him that the speaker believes that $p$; motives which the speaker neither achieves nor believes to have achieved through such a convincing procedure. I repeat that I do not doubt that the desire to convince the addressee is also a frequent motive; but in view of this rich sample of motives, we still are in need of an explanation for choosing one to be the ultimate source of conventional meaning.

Two rejoinders seem to be natural:[93] In every such case, either the speaker in fact had the intentions (contrary to appearances), or he did not in fact state (report, claim etc,) that $p$. Let us consider each in turn.

I do not find the first rejoinder too promising. For unless the existence of the above cases is simply denied, one would have to assume

---

93) They were in fact raised by Andreas Kemmerling (in discussion).

two motives — my salient but allegedly superficial one, and one that is hidden but allegedly operative. However, given the way in which I have told my stories, the superficial motives seem to fully account for the utterances, whereas the hidden motive (of convincing the addressee) would lack explanatory value. We must not confuse something like explanatory value in general (very often, speakers intend to convince; in a sense, this is why their utterances have their meanings) with explanatory value in particular cases (speakers state what they state because they want to convince). But the latter is what we need in order to attribute the motives in particular cases.

The second rejoinder should arouse our suspicion. Everyone who would suggest that the speakers say things different from those which I take them to be saying will be defending a theory which forces him to do so. Ask a Gricean what the meanings of my speakers' utterances are. Using pencil and paper, he will construct them from the intentions which may be attributed to the speakers. Of course, intuitions may be guided by theories; but they may be distorted as well.

## § 31 Gricean intentions: Irrelevant and unlikely

In acknowledging that the desire to convince the addressee is a frequent motive for speakers in making constative utterances, I did not want to acknowledge that Gricean intentions are frequent.[94] Of course, nothing prevents speakers from having the rest of Gricean intentions in cases where the first intention is clearly present (i.e. the speaker wanting to convince his addressee of the pertinent fact). But what happens when the speaker either does not care whether the addressee recognizes this intention or does not care about whether the addressee's key to acquiring the respective belief comes from recognizing his intention? I shall argue two points: First, that there is nothing fishy or non−standard about an utterance if one or both intentions are lacking; and second, that in most cases they are in fact likely to be missing. If the speaker neither intends for his addressee to recognize his desire to convince him nor intends his

---

94) My criticism will challenge the second Gricean intention, i.e. that the speaker must intend that the addressee recognizes that the speaker intends to convince him. Therefore, this criticism applies equally if one accepts Bennett's reconstruction of the third intention where the speaker need only rely on (rather than intend) this recognition to be the addressee's clue (*Linguistic Behaviour*, p. 125). It also applies to Kemmerling's substantial re−modelling of Grice's leading ideas (in 'Was Grice mit "meinen" meint' and 'Utterer's Meaning Revisited'). For Kemmerling postulates too that the speaker goes on the assumption that the addressee recognizes his motive, although in his definition there is not just one condition which states the requirement.

addressee not to recognize his desire, can he nevertheless intend to convince him by utterances? Of course he can; he may simply rely on his addressee understanding the conventional meaning of his utterance. This kind of reliance does not add up to much; it is a normal acquired disposition of any native speaker. It will typically manifest itself in cases of misunderstanding. In such instances, the speaker is astonished by the fact that the addressee has failed to grasp what he *said* rather than what he *meant*, because for him − as a native speaker − grasping what he said seems to be easier for any other native speaker than grasping what he meant.

One could argue that a speaker who wants to convince his addressee with his utterance cannot simply rely on his addressee's understanding what he has said; in addition, he must rely on the assumption that his addressee believes (1) that he chose the correct expression (i.e. that he said what he meant), (2) that he is honest (i.e. is convinced himself), and (3) that he is well − informed (i.e. is rightly convinced). The first of these three supplements will be relevant for our present purposes if we go on the supposition that a speaker who relies on the fact that his addressee believes that he (the speaker) meant what he said *ipso facto* intends for the addressee to recognize what he meant. − I cite these three together because their conjunction nicely manifests a rationalistic bias which I happen not to share. I find no fault with speakers who, in trying to convince their addressees with an utterance which is a report that $p$, are not prepared for any of the three corresponding challenges. They show some trust that they can reach their goal (convince the addressee) through certain means (giving the report) which may seem unadvisably naive to those people who think that in order to be rational you must be addicted to reasoning. In the first place, I see no reason at all why people should cease to be competent speakers on account of their being naive. But aside from this, I also see no naivety in relying on conclusions without relying on sets of premises from which they follow. Let us take the speaker's subjective probability of the addressee's being convinced of $p$, relative to his understanding the conventional meaning of his report that $p$, to be 0.95; this no doubt will increase if the speaker further believes that the addressee believes that he meant what he said, that he is honest, and well − informed. However, the speaker may still stick to 0.95 because he has no opinion on these further matters; and this is anything but irrational.

If the speaker does not need to *rely* on the addressee's recognizing his intention to convince him − let alone *intend* him to recognize this −

then we need not worry about whether the speaker wishes for the addressee to use this recognition as a key to the fact which he is to be convinced of. I see no reason at all for such a requirement (for utterances with a conventional meaning, *nota bene*!), and I am happy that I don't have to discuss this.

However, since it is possible to describe empirical evidence that would in fact warrant the ascription of Gricean intentions it might well be the case that though unnecessary in principle, they are actually present in most cases where speakers say something with a conventional meaning. I don't believe this. Our language is an established conventional language. (I am stating this in order to assure agreement, not to convince my readers.) For the moment, then, we need not quarrel about what its conventionality consists in, but instead may use its speakers as examples of speakers using a conventional language. Now if in our language a speaker makes an utterance with the conventional meaning of a report that $p$ (i.e. if he reports that $p$), this will have a conventional result (at the moment we will not argue about the character of this result). Above and beyond its conventional result, making the utterance will also have a natural effect in a fairly large set of contexts — the addressee will be convinced of $p$. We could speculate on why this is the case, but the explanation is not important: we simply note the fact. We may further-more agree that in acquiring their language, speakers learn that in giving reports they produce this natural effect. It is just as likely that they will continue to use this acquired knowledge in giving reports in order to convince people, as it is that they will use their acquired knowledge that water flows from a tap if they turn it on in order to fill a glass. In the latter case, their intention to fill the glass accounts sufficiently for their behavior (granted the bit of knowledge); as does their intention to convince the addresseee in the former case. I know of no empirical evidence which actually requires us to ascribe a more complicated intention in such normal cases.

## § 32 Speakers' meaning and conventional utterance meaning: Empirically connected

In the previous section my attempt to discredit the relevance of what the speaker means for what he says was restricted in two ways: First, I discussed only Gricean intentions (for the reason that no other ones are being offered as sources of meaning). Second, I left conventional meaning unspecified (to avoid question − begging argument). In the present section, I hope to launch a more effective attack against the doctrine that 'meaning is where something is meant', by arguing, first, from what I take to be a more down — to — earth concept of speaker's meaning, viz. what he wants to say rather than what he wants to communicate, and second, from the concept of conventional utterance meaning explained above, viz. the utterance's conventional result.

Stating it broadly and leaving it open to attack, my central claim is the following: (1) What a speaker, who speaks without deviating from his convention, means in a single case is irrelevant for what he says (for the conventional meaning of his utterance). (2) There is no conceptual link, though a strong empirical one, between the conventional meanings of utterances, on the one hand, and speakers generally meaning what they say, on the other. (3) There is no conceptual link, though a strong empirical one of a different kind, between our having a certain kind of conventional language, on the one hand, and speakers generally speaking from the motives they speak from, on the other.

I shall briefly and crudely deal with the first point. Everyone knows that with an utterance one can say things which one does not mean and can fail to say things one does mean — recall slips of the tongue, using wrong names, misconstruing the utterance situation and so on. In such cases, we continue to be parties to our language conventions — this is precisely why we say things we do not mean. I do not dispute that there are cases where the error is so much out in the open that hearers are not entitled to pin the speaker down on what he would otherwise have said; by convention, his utterance then has either the openly intended meaning or no definite meaning at all. Even in such cases, however, it is not the speaker's intention that makes his intended meaning the conventional meaning, but rather a special trouble — shooting convention which is useful in distributing the burden of avoiding misunderstandings; and it is a convention for marginal cases. (There is a different convention for cases where the speaker declares what he means; see § 35 below.)

The main conceptual point here is this: If we want to answer the question about what a speaker meant with his utterance, we have to use procedures which differ from those required for answering the question as to what he said. In the first case, we have to inquire into his intention; in the second case, we must know what he uttered under what circumstances as well as the utterance meaning rules of his language. Therefore, asking what a speaker meant is sensible without previously specifying a language he may have used; asking what he said is not. If we want to find out what a speaker meant, we will be greatly *aided* if we know his mother tongue; finding out what he said always *means* finding out what he said in a given language.

A speaker who means what he says has the intention of producing the conventional result of his utterance. That one actually produces a conventional result of an utterance through making the utterance *with* the intention of producing this result does not mean that *due to* the intention one produces the result by making the utterance. Likewise, driving a bolt in by turning it *with* the intention of driving it in does not mean that *due to* the intention of driving it in, one drives it in by turning it. Conventional languages are there and any speaker is invited to use them. He can use them unintentionally or intentionally. But the language does not become useable by the speaker intentionally using it.

For my second claim, we need to think about the most frequent intentions of all or most speakers. Let us imagine that it happens too frequently that too many spakers do not intend to say what they in fact say. I do not know how to specify 'too many' or 'too frequently'; but admitting the very 'too' means granting a point against me, so I need not bother. Admitting it boils down to saying that there is a threshold below which the system collapses. For example, in circumstances where according to the utterance meaning rules of their language, uttering $u$ is a report that $p$, too often too many speakers do not have the intention to and therefore (granting 'therefore' is granting a big step) are not prepared to take responsibility for $p$ to obtain. They will come up against sanctions. But if there are too many careless speakers, they will feel encouraged to oppose sanctions (this is an empirical hypothesis I grant), and on their own part, they will not apply sanctions if roles are exchanged (I grant also this empirical hypothesis). Issuing and tolerating sanctions will no longer be *en vogue*; uttering $u$ in the relevant circumstances will no longer commit the speaker to take responsibility for $p$ to obtain. The utterance meaning rule has become obsolete. Generally speaking, if it happens too often that too many native speakers of a language do not mean what they say, then for empirical reasons the language will change or even die out.

Now to my third and last claim. A speaker who means what he says and therefore makes his utterance intentionally will generally have some motive for his utterance. What kind of aims can be achieved by using a language will, of course, depend on what this language is like. One can drive a bolt in with the intention of driving it in in order to mount a wheel on a car; by the same intentional use of this tool, one will not succeed in tacking two boards together for preparing a mitre joint. Thus there is a connection between what the language is like and the motives from which to use it. In conceding most of my battlefield, I will concern myself only with the motive of convincing people. In reporting that $p$, how can we convince people that $p$ is the case? Well, in reporting that $p$, we take the responsibility upon ourselves; we become reliable because we must avoid paying damages. Because we are reliable, our reports are usually true, i.e. people who rely on them are usually not disappointed. Therefore they are accustomed to believe us. If we use a decision theoretical framework of belief, the mechanism of convincing is even more direct: Addressees are convinced of $p$ to a high enough degree to rely on $p$ because by taking the responsibility on ourselves we minimize their risk.

But let us look at how this works. Because our utterances have their conventional results, they can be used for achieving our motives. It is not the case that the basis for our utterances' being reports consists in our motive to convince. In stressing this fact, I am prepared to admit that our language would look quite different, unless we were constantly using it for convincing our addressees − it would look different because it would be a totally different system of rules for utterance meaning. If we were not continuously informing fellow people of facts which they have not seen our life, of course, would be very different; in particular, there would be at most an extremely small accumulation of knowledge in passing from generation to generation (restricted to things that one can show or model). Maybe we would be living somewhere in Middle Stone Age. Of course we would have a different language (if at all). The fact, then, that we use our language for convincing is co − responsible for our having precisely the language we have. To put it more dangerously − this fact is co − responsible for our language being what it is; less dangerously − for our having survived in the way we did with such a language.

Sexual intercourse has certain physiological and psychological bases. These bases are not what they are because they are used for the pursuit of happiness. On the contrary, they are so used because they are what they are. Nevertheless, we would miss them if we were not constantly using them for the pursuit of happiness − for the simple reason of having died out.

§ 33 The Thomistic fallacy

I have tried to argue that any 'meaning is where something is meant' explication of conventional linguistic meaning is wrong, and that there is

94

a better kind of explication. If my contention is correct then any hint as to why the incorrect type of explication is so obviously attractive would be welcome. (Its attractiveness is beyond doubt.) Therefore I shall draw attention to some facts that seem to explain at least part of the attractiveness of the explication that 'meaning is where something is meant'. If this explication is correct, these facts would have proven to have been heuristically fruitful. If it is incorrect, they point to a possible diagnosis.

There are many concepts in ordinary language which are similar to the concept of conventional linguistic meaning, (1) in that they are perfectly reputable (if we disregard the misgivings of some perpetually complaining philosophers) and are constantly used in sensible talk, and (2) in that they are intimately connected with some kind or kinds of intentional activity such that these intentional activities could be seen as the bases for the concepts in question. Let us begin with some down−to−earth examples: A building is something which people have built with the intention to build it (or at any rate with the intention to build something); a natural collection of caves used as a monastery is not a building. A garden may look as natural as one wants − but unless the word is used metaphorically, it must have come about and be preserved by some kind of gardening. The following are more akin to our case: an actor's role, which is whatever the author or director want him to play; and the purpose of a pressure group, which is determined by certain intentions of its members. It is often said that the purpose of a given law is what the legislator wants to achieve by it (there are problems here though). And it may be said that in a given group there are no values, unless its members value them − although here we must be careful to use 'to value' in a very broad sense in which valuing something may be manifested in the most varied ways.

The concept of conventional linguistic meaning resembles such concepts. It is perfectly reputable and can be used in sensible speech; and it is intimately connected with an intentional activity, viz. speakers' making their utterances and thereby meaning what their utterances conventionally mean. Therefore, if we want to explain why the concept of conventional linguistic meaning is reputable (for some motive or other − say for quieting some perpetually complaining philosophers), it seems promising to explain it in terms of the intentional activity of making an utterance and thereby meaning what the utterance conventionally means.

However, there is no guarantee that every such concept which is intimately connected with some intentional activity is somehow founded on this activity. For instance, there is an intimate connection between the fact that a convention of scientists agrees on a standard and the further fact that this standard becomes conventional. However, a standard may be conventional without ever having been agreed upon explicitly. In the same way, if all concerned want to further the purpose of an institution, the institution's purpose will be what they want to further; if every godfather tries to be a good godfather, then the role of a godfather is what every godfather tries to be. However, the purpose of an institution as well as a social role cannot normally be explained in terms of people's furthering this purpose or in terms of their trying to play this role. If every group member ranks all group members in the same way ('ranking' to be taken in the narrow sense of acts of ranking), the ranks of the group members will correspond to how they rank each other; but they may have ranks without there being any acts of ranking at all. History of philosophy and history of science have seen ill—advised enterprises posit such connections: arguing from the obvious order in nature to the existence of someone's ordering nature's affairs, or from the indisputable appropriateness pervading the organic would either to the existence of someone who has created it for his own purposes (as with St. Thomas);[95] or to that of eerie entities which, as the organisms' entelechies, make them appropriate for themselves ( as with Driesch).[96]

There may even be one and the same word on both sides. For example, we can *make* something so that it achieves a certain *making*; but it may have a *making* without having been *made*. And, moreover, there may be both the same word and the overall coextensiveness which (as I admitted in § 32) characterizes conventional utterance meaning and speakers' meaning : normally, piano tuners tune a piano so that it has *the* piano tuning; if they all stopped doing this, the piano tuning would probably cease to be what it is. But the piano tuning is not what it is because piano tuners stick to it; they stick to it because it is what it is.

I do in fact think that the explication that 'meaning is where something is meant' is Thomistic in this sense. It explains a social fact, conventional linguistic meaning, which is intimately connected to a kind of intentional individual behavior, and it explains it as due to the latter behavior. But wrongly so. If I am wrong about the correctness of the explication, then being Thomistic has proved successful in this case.

## § 34 Genitivus subjectivus and genitivus objectivus

From the point of view of translation into German, the English verb 'to mean' is ambiguous. Where it is used with a personal subject (a

---

95) *Summa Theologica*, Ia, Quaestio 2,3.
96) *Philosophie des Organischen*, Leipzig ⁴1928, pp. 126f.

speaker), it has to be rendered by 'meinen', whereas with other subjects (utterances, sentences, words; or measle spots) the correct translation is 'bedeuten'. Now this could be just an insignificant idiosyncrasy of German; it would be a real ambiguity, and a dangerous one, if the 'meaning is where something is meant' explication were incorrect. For the expression 'utterance $u$ means $m$' would then serve to obscure the distinction in the following way:

By the standard passive transformation, 'the speaker of $u$ means $m$ by $u$' can be paraphrased as '$m$ is meant by $u$ by the speaker of $u$'. Now since whoever means anything by $u$ is the speaker of $u$, he may be dropped without loss of information: '$m$ is meant by $u$'. If we now apply the inverse of the passive transformation, we end up with: '$u$ means $m$'. For this reason 'the spaker of $u$ means $m$ by $u$' can be condensed to '$u$ means $m$'. Such abbreviations are quite common, of course, where there is a word for the result of the agent's action which can replace the word for his action (as 'by the utterance' can replace 'by uttering what is uttered'): 'The murderer killed Sister George by a stroke' becomes ' a stroke killed Sister George' etc.

However, we should not overlook the following: If the gerund, 'the meaning of the utterance', is used to replace 'what the utterance means', then whereas the latter expression can in fact designate what the speaker means (in the condensed version), the gerund cannot. For in 'the meaning of the utterance', the genitive definitely is *genitivus subjectivus* while it would have to be *genitivus objectivus* in order to designate what the speaker means, because this would be the only possibility of interpreting 'meaning' as the gerund of the verb 'to mean' which is transitive. If we compare 'the boiling of the soup' or 'the turning of the ship', we find that in the case of *genitivus objectivus* both 'boiling' and 'turning' are gerunds of the transitive forms of the verbs 'to boil' and 'to turn'; in the case of *genitivus subjectivus*, they are gerunds of the intransitive forms of the same verbs.

If by 'the tuning of the piano' we refer to the overall musical fact (a social fact), the genitive is *genitivus subjectivus*, as with 'the meaning of the utterance'. In interpreting 'of the piano' as *genitivus objectivus* the expression refers to an episode of somebody tuning a certain piano rather than to the social fact. If we let 'his meaning of the utterance' (or 'speaker's meaning') have *genitivus objectivus*, we end up with an episode of somebody meaning something but not with what he means.

To repeat: If the 'meaning is where something is meant' explication is correct, then jumping from *genitivus objectivus* to *genitivus subjectivus* and back is heuristically fruitful, though frivolous. If it is incorrect, frivolity has been given its due punishment.

## § 35 Declarations of meaning

Utterances may be less clear than is desirable for purposes of communication, and for such cases languages are well advised to stock up on remedies. For example, if the addressee does not understand the speaker, he might say "Cancel". This would serve to undo the speaker's utterance, and unless he tries again he would be held to have said nothing. Or the addressee might say "You yean such and such". This would impute some unambiguous interpretation to the speaker who would then be held to have said what the addressee said that he yeant. A friendlier convention might give him the right to say "Cancel" if the addressee went too far.

Such conventions would favor the addressee who has an easy way out, while the speaker must watch out when he expresses himself. Our conventions are different. They favor the speaker who has an easy way out by saying "No, I didn't mean that". If he says this then what he said does not count. Or, he may say: "I mean ...", "I meant ...". If he does this, then what he said to mean or to have meant by his preceding utterance counts as this preceding utterance's meaning. It is not quite clear, to me at least, under which circumstances the addressee has a right to reject such retractations or reinterpretations as going too far by saying something like "Cancel", viz.: "But you *did* say it" or: "You cannot possibly have meant *that*". On the whole, with us, speakers have a high degree of authority on how their utterances are to be interpreted if they deliver a corresponding declaration. This observation is due to Wittgenstein (the passage concerns the parallel question about the content of an image):

> "If you want to know whom he meant, ask him. ... And his answer would be  decisive." (*PI* II iii, *p.* 177$^e$)

Here emphasis is to be put on 'decisive'. If his answer makes a *decision* about whom he has been referring to then it is not a *report* on whom he has been referring to; rather it subsequently makes his former utterance an utterance about the person whose name he gives in answering the question. That he can do this is, of course, guaranteed by our conventions — which could be different.

So there is a certain conventional prerogative for the speaker to determine what he says by declaring what he means. In accordance with this convention, we will often ask him what he means; since his answer to this question settles the question as to what he has said, what he means seems conventionally to determine what he says. This, however, is not the case. In such instances, what he says is determined by what he *declares he means* (or meant), not by what he *means*. Even if we have strong reasons to suppose that in making his first utterance he meant something different, we grant him the right to authoritatively interpret his own utterances. The conventional force is not with meaning; it is with declarations of meaning. And even there it need not be.

# Chapter VI
# The same case for sentence meaning: NIVEAU

## § 36 The new problem

As we have seen in our investigation of NIVEAU zero, using a language for saying things in the full−blooded sense of 'saying' − i.e. making utterances with conventional meanings − does not depend on the language having sentence meanings. In NIVEAU zero, there are no sentence meanings because none of its signs have a meaning, the simple reason being this: Rules which specify utterance meanings do so without taking into account any differences between the signs which are used; since they succeed in doing this, it would be idle to posit meanings to signs.

However, illuminating as it may be to learn that we can utter something meaningful without using a meaningful sign, we are much more interested in how we come to say something by using meaningful sentences − as we are accustomed to when we speak English, for instance. We shall presently see that this is a rather complicated matter; in any case much more complicated than is suggested by the picture of someone who utters a sentence which means that it is raining and who thereby states that it is raining. There are, in fact, two questions about this picture: First, what it means for a sentence to have a given meaning; and second, how the meaning of a sentence contributes to the meanings of its utterances.

I shall try to attack both of these questions by returning to NIVEAU. Up until now, we have restricted our considerations to the use of horn and beams, i.e. to the fragment NIVEAU zero. If we try to describe all of NIVEAU, we shall see that we cannot do without positing sentence meanings because we need entities which, in a certain way, contribute to the meanings of utterances. This will answer both our questions at once; for sentence meanings will then be precisely those entities which are best fit for contributing what is required.

In our enterprise, we can continue to use NIVEAU as a case study because it differs from NIVEAU zero in what for the present context is a decisive feature: NIVEAU contains signs which are not interchangeable. This means, first of all, that there are additional ways of signalling in NIVEAU, i.e. additional patterns of behavior for which the following points hold:

(1) They lead to conventional deviations that can be construed as results of meaningful utterances.

(2) They connect utterance situations with utterance meanings via rules all of which can be easily stated for each such behavioral pattern taken separately.

(3) They are good candidates for constituting signalling behavior according to our tentative list in § 19.

Some examples are the stopping gesture, the beckoning gesture and the direction gesture, the right and left blinker, and nodding and shaking one's head. ( For a complete list, see Appendix II.) Also, certain driving maneuvers can be used as signs. (On these, compare § 37.) The easiest way of covering utterance meanings which are generated by these patterns of behavior would consist in simply enlarging our list of ways of signalling while retaining our set of utterance meaning rules, thus treating all ways of signalling as interchangeable. However, this is impossible for two reasons.

In the first place, the additional patterns of behavior do not have the utterance meanings predicted by the rules of NIVEAU zero in every case when they are used in the place of horn honking or beam flashing. For instance, although the right blinker can be used to offer a driver who is up ahead to change his lane, it cannot be used for offering an oncoming driver to turn left (while horn and beam can).

In the second place, almost all of the 'newcomers' can be used to generate additional utterance meanings. Here 'additional' covers three different facts:

(1) The utterance meanings do not occur in NIVEAU zero at all. There are two such cases: informing whether or not $p$, and informing that $p$. (In NIVEAU zero, there is only informing when it is the case that $p$; see rule (14), App. I.)

(2) The utterance meanings occur in NIVEAU zero. However, if in NIVEAU they are generated by the use of 'newcomers', this may happen in circumstances which are completely different from those which are necessary in NIVEAU zero. Almost every utterance meaning in NIVEAU zero is generated in situations which are dominated by salient interests; in NIVEAU such interests are unnecessary for some requests, as well as for informing that $p$. The precise details will become clear from rules which will eventually be stated for NIVEAU. In the meantime, situations which are not dominated by salient interests will be called 'inconspicuous'. NIVEAU zero requires situations which are dominated by salient interests; NIVEAU can function in inconspicuous situations too.

(3) In both NIVEAU zero and NIVEAU, the utterance meanings occur in about the same circumstances. However, if the utterance meanings are generated by the use of 'newcomers' in place of beam flashing or horn honking, the situation may lack a feature which is essential in NIVEAU zero. To give examples: S may offer A to slip into the line in front of him by flashing his beams *if he leaves a gap*; if he uses the direction gesture instead ('waves A into the line'), *leaving a gap is unnecessary* and A may enter in as soon as the gap opens up. Or S may turn down A's request to let him enter in by honking his horn *if he pulls up to the car ahead*. If he uses the stopping gesture instead, *pulling up is unnecessary*. In the rules of NIVEAU, we will see which circumstances become irrelevant if beam flashing or horn honking are replaced by 'newcomers'. In the meantime, let us call them 'helpful' circumstances. Whereas NIVEAU zero requires helpful circumstances, NIVEAU instead sometimes does with specific signs. To simply construe our newcomers as additional ways of signalling while retaining the rules of NIVEAU zero would thus result in an incomplete description of NIVEAU.

Unless our future rules distinguish between different ways of signalling, they will be both incorrect and incomplete. Any set of rules that is to represent a correct and complete system of the utterance meanings of NIVEAU must therefore distinguish between different ways of signalling. This means that we meet with a new kind of difference between two ways of signalling. Beam flashing and horn honking are, of course, different; after all one is optical, the other acoustical. However, they do not need to be distinguished by the rules which generate utterance meanings; thus they do not differ with respect to their serviceability for producing utterance meanings. On the other hand, using the left blinker and flashing one's beams do not only look different; they also differ with respect to their serviceability for producing utterance meanings.

'$x$ and $y$ differ with respect to their serviceability for producing utterance meanings' is not a very apt expression, of course. Why not simply say that they differ in meaning? The answer is simple: Whereas we have explained what it is for an utterance to have a meaning, i.e. what it means that *using a way of signalling in a certain kind of situation* has an utterance meaning, we have not yet explained what it might mean for *a way of signalling* to have a meaning. (Whatever such a meaning might be, it would definitely not be an utterance meaning.) Later on, we shall indeed see that, as soon as ways of signalling differ with respect to their serviceability for producing utterance meanings, we can (1) explain what it is for a way of signalling to have a meaning ('meaning' in a new sense, different from the sense of 'utterance meaning'), (2) show that ways of signalling have a meaning in this new sense, and (3) show that if they differ with respect to their serviceability for producing utterance meanings, they differ in meaning in the new sense. Making use of this future result, from this point on I shall say that our ways of signalling differ in meaning. Since what has a meaning or what differs in meaning from something else is usually called a sign (provided we are not referring to utterance meaning), I shall call our ways of signalling 'signs' and shall drop 'signalling' in favor of 'using a sign' or 'uttering a sign'.

Therefore, our task can be stated in the following way: We have to find rules for utterance meanings which are sensitive to differences in the meanings of those signs which are used.

## § 37 Grouping signs by positing new entities

For a while, let us forget about those driving maneuvers which are used as signs in NIVEAU. We then have a determinate number of signs (twenty if interchangeable ones are each counted separately, sixteen if they are handled like allomorphs of one sign). Just as we started our entire case study by restricting our attention to beam flashing and horn honking, we might carry out fifteen further case studies, restricting each one to a different sign. We would end up with a sixteen – chapter description of NIVEAU, one chapter for each sign. Each chapter would contain a couple of rules stating the utterance meanings that result from using, under different circumstances, the sign which is the focus of that chapter.

We would soon realize that there would be a host of repetitions; many rules would reoccur in each chapter. Under these circumstances, it would perhaps be profitable to have only two chapters, the first one listing these rules and stating those signs for which each rule holds, the second one listing rules that state pecularities of the use of some signs. (If lucky, we would not come across any such pecularities.) This would amount to *grouping the signs, by listing them, according to how they can be used to say things.*

A similar thing could happen when the leader of a scout troup (with six members) distributes work one evening. It would be tedious to tell each individual scout what he is to do: "Ann, you help me put up the tent. Betty, you are on water duty. Christopher, you gather wood for the bonfire. David, you're to help me put up the tent. Emily, go get firewood. Fred, you are on water duty." Instead, he may say: "Emily and Christopher, you gather firewood. Fred and Betty, you two are on water duty. David and Anna, help me put up the tent." He has now *grouped the scouts, by listing them, according to what they are to do.*

He might also have achieved the very same grouping in another way. And if asked why he had distributed the three tasks in just this way, he might explain his grouping, with something like the following: "I asked David and Anna to help me with the tent because they are the biggest; I asked Emily and Christopher to gather firewood because they are the smallest; and I sent Fred and Betty for water because they are in between." Thus his grouping might have been: The biggest ones help me with the tent; the smallest ones gather firewood; and those in between are on water duty. That is, he would *group his scouts according to those properties which make them suitable for the different tasks.*

In just the same way *we can group our signs,* not by listing them, but *by way of those features which make them suitable for producing utterance meanings according to utterance meaning rules.* The first procedure — grouping by listing — is only possible in cases where the number of things to be grouped is determinate. However, I shall try to show that the usual standards of intelligent theorizing would require us to group signs by their suitability features (rather than by listing them), even if the number of signs were determinate. This is why at the moment I am neglecting driving maneuvers which are signs; for their number is not determinate, and this fact prohibits grouping by listing anyway.

It is rather obvious that the bigger children are more suited to help with the tent. But what features of a sign make it suitable for producing utterance meanings? This, of course, depends on what the utterance meaning rules look like. Let us start with those of NIVEAU zero and assess the following findings:

Let us consider situations which (a) are like those where rule (2) (for offering) applies, except that neither beam flashing nor horn honking are used and that the speaker $S$ fails to do something suitable with regard to what he offers (i.e. the 'helpful' circumstance is missing), and in which (b) $S$ offers the addressee $A$ to let him do $V$, and does this by using one of three signs: the direction gesture, the beckoning gesture, or the right blinker. What we find out about such situations is this:

| When $S$, in offering $A$ to let him do $V$, has used the | then it was suitable for $A$'s doing $V$ |
|---|---|
| direction gesture | *that A moves in the direction indicated* |
| beckoning gesture | *that A approaches S* |
| right blinker | *that S intends to turn right* |

This is far from exciting. But now let us consider situations which (a) are like those where rule (5) (for requesting) applies, except that neither beam flashing nor horn honking are used, and in which (b) $S$ requests $A$ to do $V$, and does this by using the direction gesture, the beckoning gesture, or the right blinker. What we find out about such situations may be somewhat more exciting:

| When $S$, in requesting $A$ to do $V$, has used the | then it was suitable for (or a possible motive for $S$'s interest in) $A$'s doing $V$ |
| --- | --- |
| direction gesture | *that A moves in the direction indicated* |
| beckoning gesture | *that A approaches S* |
| right blinker | *that S intends to turn right* |

If we are audacious, we can now venture the following moves: First, we attribute what is denoted by the italicized 'that' — clauses to the respective signs; what is thus attributed to a sign we call that sign's 'suitability marker', or '$sm$'. Second, we extend rules (2) and (5) of NIVEAU zero in such a way that they cover, on the one hand, the same situations as those covered up until now, and on the other hand, situations where a sign other than horn honking or beam flashing is used and where this sign's $sm$ fits the situation in a way which is specific for each rule. (2) and (5) of NIVEAU zero then become $(2a)^{97)}$ and (5a):

(2a) By failing to do $U$, $x$ prevents $y$ from doing $V$; $x$ has more claim to omit doing $U$ than $y$ does have to do $V$. Now either $x$ flashes his beams/honks his horn and does something suitable for $U$, or $x$ uses a sign with an $sm$ which is suitable for $U$. Thereby, $x$ offers $y$ to do $U$.

(5a) By failing to do $V$, $y$ prevents $x$ from doing $U$. Now either $x$ flashes his beams/honks his horn, or $x$ uses a sign with an $sm$ which is suitable for $y$'s doing $V$ or a possible motive for $x$'s interest in $V$. Thereby, $x$ requests of $y$ that $y$ do $V$.

The effect of these moves is this: We have posited features for the signs which, *in connection with suitable utterance meaning rules*, make them fit for producing utterance meanings. The grouping of signs which is necessary for each rule is achieved, not by a sign's $sm$, but by a relation between the sign's $sm$ and the concrete utterance situation.

The above moves are not necessary at all and we can do without them. But they can be judged with regard to their theoretical fruitfulness: The more rules of NIVEAU zero which can be adjusted in the manner

---

97) (1a) and (2a) are provisional formulations of the final NIVEAU rules.

described, and the more signs for which we find *sms* which fit all these rules, the greater the theoretical fruitfulness of each case of positing an *sm*. As the complete description of NIVEAU in Appendix II will show, we can in fact use the *sms* so forcefully that grouping the signs by listing them would be dreadfully ad hoc, even if possible in principle. This can be seen if we consider how, in using this strategy, we can cope with additional utterance meanings, viz. requests and information that *p*, in inconspicuous situations, i.e. situations which are not dominated by salient interests.

Let us consider inconspicuous situations where the speaker either uses the direction gesture or the beckoning gesture or his right blinker. What are the utterance meanings?

| use, in inconspicuous situations, | has the utterance meaning that |
|---|---|
| of the direction gesture | *S* requests of *A* that *A* moves in the direction indicated |
| of the beckoning gesture | *S* requests of *A* that *A* approaches *S* |
| of the right blinker | *S* informs *A* that *S* intends to turn right[98] |

Look what has happened: We want to attribute certain *sms* to our signs in order to understand why they are suited for producing utterance meanings, similar to utterance meanings we have encountered in NIVEAU zero, in situations which are similar to ones we are familiar with from NIVEAU zero. And exactly the same *sms* show up in further utterance meanings which are produced by using the same signs; however, some of these utterance meanings are completely unfamiliar to us from NIVEAU zero, and the others, even if familiar, are produced in inconspicuous situations, whereas in NIVEAU zero their production depended on salient interests.

Thus we can try to state a rule for NIVEAU which generates such utterance meanings according to the *sm* of a sign which is used in an inconspicuous situation. If we succeed in doing this, our previous *sm*–attributions will thereby pass a further examination for theoretical fruitfulness. Stating the required rule turns out to be extremely easy, as is seen from the matrix below. In the left column are listed those signs which can be used *in inconspicuous situations* to generate utterance meanings in a manner which we are unfamiliar with from NIVEAU zero. In the right column the utterance meanings are given; the italicized 'that'

---

98) This is not quite correct and will be amended in § 38.

clauses denote *exactly those sms* which, via the slightly revised NIVEAU zero rules (to be stated in Appendix II), make the sign suitable to account for utterance meanings which the rules can be used to produce *in salient interests situations.*

| In inconspicuous situations, by using the | |
| --- | --- |
| | *S requests of A* |
| stopping gesture | *that A does not approach S* |
| direction gesture | *that A moves in the direction indicated* |
| beckoning gesture | *that A approches S* |
| slowing down gesture | *that A slows down* |
| blue flashing light, police sirene | *that A keeps away from S* |
| | *S informs A* |
| right blinker | *that S intends to turn right*[99] |
| left blinker | *that S intends to turn left*[99] |
| warning blinker | *that S is an obstacle* |
| warning triangle | *that there is danger ahead* |

The utterance meaning's proposition is straightforwardly identical with the sign's *sm*; thus all we need is an element which determines the illocutionary force. This is quite easy to find: if the *sm* is that *A* does something, we have a request; and an information if the *sm* is that *p*, for some *p* other than that *A* does something. Our *sm* — approach thus passes its second exam for theoretical fruitfulness with an *A* +. Let us put it to a third test, with new signs.

Driving maneuvers normally have normal purposes, and normally they are fully understandable in light of these purposes. However, some feature of a maneuver may not be understandable in this way. Or, in contrast, some feature may be missing for the maneuver to be understood. Understood in light of its normal purpose, there is either too much or too little about the maneuver. Precisely these kinds of maneuvers function as signs in NIVEAU: Maneuvers which are signs of NIVEAU are those which are either executed in an exaggerated fashion or which are started and curtailed at once. For instance, the following are exaggerated maneuvers: Leaving a huge gap for someone to slip in instead of leaving a sufficiently large gap, or moving to the far right much earlier than is necessary to enable an oncoming driver to pass a

---

99) This is not quite correct and will be amended in § 38.

narrowing in his lane. (Both may be used as offers.) Maneuvers which are started and curtailed at once include for instance: Rolling forward one meter to a line up and stopping ("Let me enter"), or weaving in and out behind a slow car ("Let me pass you").

If a driving maneuver $M$ is either executed in an exaggerated manner or if it is started and curtailed at once, I shall call it a 'performance' of $M$. Thus performances of driving maneuvers are signs of NIVEAU. This is an empirical hypothesis which cannot be exhaustively confirmed, for everybody can invent new signs of this kind. And this is why there can be no definite inventory of NIVEAU's signs; the inventory is indefinite although there is no syntax. Any language may lack a syntax while rejoicing in an indefinite number of signs; this is because there are more ways of identifying members of open classes than just by the rules of syntax. In the case of NIVEAU, the identification is achieved by iconicity, and for distinguishing different iconic signs from one another it is sufficient to distinguish different normal driving maneuvers from one another.

Given that we cannot list the driving maneuvers[100] which are signs of NIVEAU, it is not only cumbersome and ad hoc, but even theoretically impossible to write NIVEAU up in chapters, dedicating one to each sign. Here our $sm-$approach has to enter its third exam for theoretical fruitfulness: For every driving maneuver which is a sign, we have to define an $sm$ which is, by the slightly revised NIVEAU rules, suitable for generating the utterance meanings which are in fact to be found, and which is determined by a general rule because we must make sure that such signs have an $sm$ even before they turn up.

The third exam is passed with flying colors: To every sign which is a performance of a driving maneuver $M$, as its $sm$ we attribute that $S$ intends $M$; and this works.

## § 38 Some semantic features: Ambiguity, negation, anaphora

In the past few sections, I have suppressed a problem about the blinkers. We can begin to consider this by noticing the following: Using them in 'inconspicuous' situations does not always mean in fact that the speaker informs the addressee that he intends to turn right or left respectively. Instead, he may sometimes inform him that he does not intend to turn left (by using the right blinker), or that he does not intend to turn right (by using the left blinker). Thus the blinkers permit two utterance

---

100) Out of convenience, I will call performances of driving maneuvers also driving maneuvers, where misunderstanding is not possible.

meanings in inconspicuous situations. In these situations, the utterance meanings of all other signs can be uniquely determined from precisely those *sms* from which utterance meanings in situations which are dominated by salient interests can be predicted in simple and systematic ways. *We want to* determine the blinkers' utterance meanings in inconspicuous situations in the same way; thus *we have to* attach two differents *sms* to each.

This move implies that there is something about inconspicuous situations that disambiguates the blinkers, and indeed there is: If it is feasible for S to move to the right (e.g. from the left lane, or at a crossing, or if he slows down as though to park etc.), then in using his right blinker in an inconspicuous situation he informs A that he intends to move to the right. If no such move is feasible (e.g. if he is parked on the right shoulder, or if he is driving in the right lane without slowing down), then in using his right blinker in an inconspicuous situation he informs A that he does not intend to move left. If we change 'right' to 'left' and vice versa we get the corresponding rule for the left blinker. We can, therefore, assign to the blinkers both of the required *sms* and assume that they are disambiguated according to whether a move to the right (left) is feasible or not.

We have to be aware, however, of the consequences which this has for the rest of our utterance meaning rules. What we want is to have any utterance meaning which results from using the blinkers in situations that are dominated by salient interests to be uniquely determined by a rule which matches the blinkers' *sms*. Since they have two *sms*, not only does one of them have to work in each case, but the blinkers also have to be disambiguated in each and every situation. And now the burden of our systematically motivated decision to regard the blinkers as ambiguous is greatly eased by the fact that if they are supposed to be disambiguated by one and the same rule in every case — by the rule cited above — then the *sm* which results for any situation will indeed fit the rules well. Had we instead been forced to assume several disambiguating mechanisms applying in different contexts, the decision would have been less easy of course; for although one requirement of ambiguity would still hold — viz. that the number of readings be finite —, two readings with one unique disambiguating device might be the most comfortable instance of a theoretically postulated ambiguity.

The impact of regarding the blinkers as ambiguous emerges most clearly from a consideration of what the alternative would be. Since the disambiguating device yields *sms* which are adequate in connections with all utterance meaning rules, it would have to be incorporated into the sets of circumstances of all these rules in order to retain its global relevance. But then it would affect the uses of all signs of NIVEAU, and this would yield incorrect utterance meanings in connection with other signs which need not be disambiguated. Thus the only way open to us would consist in devising special utterance meaning rules for the blinkers, a way which in principle is open to us anyway (for the signs which can be enumerated, see § 37), and which we refused to take for reasons of theoretical fruitfulness. Positing ambiguity comes out, then, as a matter of theory construction, not as a matter of intuitiveley imagining different readings.

There is still another theoretical reason for positing ambiguity: We need it in connection with the rudiments of negation which are to be found in NIVEAU.

Although dominated by salient interests, there is one situation which is not covered by NIVEAU zero: $A$ has a standard interest in doing $V$, but he does not know whether or not he may do $V$. $S$ knows whether or not $A$ may do V. Some examples: $A$ wants to back out of a narrow driveway. However, the traffic on the street is heavy. $S$ is standing on the sidewalk. $A$ has an interest in knowing whether or not he may back out, and $S$ knows whether he may back out. Or: On a winding overland route, a driver $A$ follows a truck which he is interested in passing. However, he cannot see how risky it would be to pass because of oncoming traffic. Thus he has an interest in knowing whether or not he may pass the truck; the truck driver $S$ knows whether $A$ may do this. If $S$ is to inform $A$, his utterance must discriminate between affirming and negating, which cannot be achieved by mere beam flashing or horn honking.

In NIVEAU, this discrimination problem is solved *by using pairs of signs*. For instance, in our first case (the driveway one) $S$ can inform $A$ that he can back out by using the beckoning gesture, and by using the stopping gesture he informs him that he cannot back out. Let us note here that this use of the gestures is neither covered by the request rule of NIVEAU zero (because $S$ need not have the slightest interest in $A$'s behavior), nor by the rule for inconspicuous situations sketched in § 37 (because the situation is dominated by salient interests). Thus we need a new rule. The first step is simple: We note that the beckoning gesture's $sm$ — that $A$ approaches $S$ — in this case implies that $A$ may back out, provided that $A$ does only what he is permitted to do. Let us abbreviate '$p$ implies that $q$, provided that everybody does only what he is permitted to do' by '$p$ lawfully implies $q$'. Then in our type of situation, $S$ might inform $A$ that $p$ (because $A$ is interested in whether or not $p$) by using a sign with an $sm$ which lawfully implies p.[101]

However, $S$ cannot use such a simple mechanism for informing $A$ that $p$ is not the case. For he can so inform him by using the stopping gesture, whereas this gesture's $sm$ — that $A$ does not approach $S$ — does not imply, lawfully or otherwise, that $A$ may not back out. To overcome this difficulty, we can make use of the fact that the stopping gesture is unambiguously related to the beckoning gesture in that both gestures' $sms$ are contradictories of each other: We assume that $S$ informs $A$ that $p$ is not the case by using a sign with an $sm$ which is the contradictory of the $sm$ of a sign whose use would mean information that $p$. In this way, signs which come in contradictory $sm$ pairs do the job of special purpose negations signs.

Although still provisional, all of this helps us to come to a description of how the blinkers can be used to give yes — no information. Let us consider the truck passing example (which frequently occurs on German overland routes). The truck driver $S$ can do one of three things: (1) He can use his left blinker and thereby inform $A$ that he may not pass him. Or (2) he can use his right blinker without slowing down and thereby inform $A$ that he may pass him without risk. Or (3) he can use his right blinker while slowing down, thereby saying nothing at all about passing. In order to account for this in accordance with our description of the driveway example, we need contradictory $sms$ for the blinkers. If we stick to our ambiguity assumption, we find these present in the first and second cases: In the first case, the left blinker's $sm$ is that $S$ intends to turn left, whereas in the second case the right blinker's $s$ is that $S$ does not intend to turn left. (Because $S$ does not slow down, it is not feasible to move to the right.) The utterance meanings come off in the following manner: The left blinker's $sm$ — that $S$ intends to turn left — lawfully implies that $A$ may not pass $S$. Because $A$ is interested in knowing whether or not he may pass $S$, he is informed that he may not. The right

---

101) Any sign's $sm$ may, of course, lawfully imply a lot of things. The fact about which $A$ is informed is singled out (1) by his standard interest in precisely this fact's obtaining, (2) by his ignorance in this respect, and (3) by the information being standardly available to $S$. For instance, the proposition that $A$ approaches $S$ implies that the transmission of $A$'s car is o.k.; however, $S$ does not standardly know whether or not this is the case, and thus he does not inform $A$ about it. And the same proposition implies that there is a distance between $S$ and $A$; however, $A$ is not standardly interested in being informed about it, and this is why he is not informed about it.

blinker's *sm*, in the second case, is the left blinker's *sm*'s contradictory. In the third case, the right blinker's *sm* is that *S* intends to turn right. This is completely irrelevant as to whether it is risky for *A* to pass *S*, and our provisional mechanism generates no utterance meaning.

Such information can also be given by nodding (or holding one's thumb up) and by shaking one's head (or waving one's hand), and this takes us to a further semantic feature, viz. anaphora. If we review the NIVEAU uses of nodding and shaking one's head, the first thing we notice is that for systematic reasons we have to assume that the signs are ambiguous.

On the one hand, *S* may nod in order to offer *A* that *S* does *V* in situations like those covered by rule (2) of NIVEAU zero (alike except for the differences which we are already familiar with by now: horn honking and beam flashing are replaced by another sign, and the 'helpful' features are missing), and he may shake his head in order to insist on his omitting *V* in situations like those covered by rule (1) of NIVEAU zero. In the successors to these rules in NIVEAU, *S*'s doing something (un)suitable for *S*'s doing *V* is replaced by the disjunction of *S*'s doing something (un)suitable and/or *S*'s using a sign with an *sm* which is (un)suitable for *S*'s doing *V*. This requires corresponding *sms* for nodding and shaking one's head; and because they are universally applicable, a good choice is to attribute the following *sms* to them:

nodding:  what *A* is interested in is the case
shaking one's head: what *A* is interested in is not the case

This attribution is useful in connection with yes—no information. Take the driveway example: In nodding, *S* informs *A* that he may back out. This is what A is interested in; thus in this case, that *A* may back out is nodding's *sm* (which trivially implies itself). In shaking his head, *S* informs *A* that he must not back out. Since *A* is interested in backing out, in this case shaking one's head has the *sm* that he must not back out.

On the other hand, *S* may nod and thereby accept *A*'s preceding offer that *A* does *V* or grant *A*'s preceding request that *S* does *V* (in situations which *mutatis mutandis* are like those covered by rules (3) and (7) of NIVEAU zero), and he may shake his head and thereby decline *A*'s preceding offer that *A* does *V* or turn down *A*'s preceding request that *S* does V (in situations which *mutatis mutandis* are like those covered by (4) and (6) of NIVEAU zero). If we put *sms* of other signs to work instead of the features which are helpful for beam flashing or horn honking, these *sms* must be suitable for *V* in the cases of accepting and granting; they must be unsuitable for $V$ in the cases of declining and turning down. Again, this requires corresponding *sm*s for nodding and shaking one's head. We obviously cannot choose the same ones as above.

Instead of trying out ad hoc strategies like distinguishing preceding offers from other preceding utterances, let us postulate that nodding and shaking one's head *are ambiguous in being either anaphorical or not.* Without a preceding utterance where $S$ was the addressee, both signs have their above−mentioned *sm*s. On the other hand, if $S$ was the addressee of a preceding utterance, then the *sm* of $S$'s nodding is *that the proposition which is part of the preceding utterance's meaning is the case*, while the *sm* of $S$'s shaking his head is *that the proposition which is part of the preceding utterance's meaning is not the case.* Note that in this case *sm*s which are neither utterance meanings nor parts of them, are defined with reference to parts of utterance meanings.

# Chapter VII
## Some results for sentence meaning

### § 39 The point of having sentence meanings

Most *sms* of the signs of NIVEAU are denoted by 'that' — clauses. This feature they share with certain things which might very naturally be called the meanings of related English or French or German sentences. When asked for the meanings of the sentences 'you do not approach me', 'tu ne t'avances pas auprès de moi', or 'du näherst dich mir nicht', a native English speaker might well reply: "The sentences mean that the addressee does not approach the speaker." When asked for the meanings of the sentences 'I intend to turn right', 'j'ai l'intention de tourner à droite', 'ich will nach rechts', he might reply: "The sentences mean that the speaker intends to turn right". (Of course, I am not referring to a linguist who has done work on semantics in one of the three languages. He perhaps would come up with beautiful trees, as an able philosopher might come up either with a bunch of brackets or with baskets full of possible worlds or something else of this kind.) Thus there seems to be a good case for saying that our *sms* occur elsewhere too, and occur there (viz. in natural languages) as sentence meanings. Can we say that we have attributed sentence meanings to the signs of NIVEAU?

I think we can. For although the signs of NIVEAU are not sentences in the sense of being syntactically structured, they have the same function in utterances as do sentences of natural languages: Using one of them under appropriate conditions is sufficient for making a meaningful utterance. Furthermore, a sign's *sm* (in NIVEAU) is what the sign contributes to the utterance meaning, just as a sentence's meaning (in a natural language) is what the sentence contributes to what is said by uttering it.

In fully developed natural languages, manners of saying something consist in uttering sentences which are not all interchangeable. If the sentences were all interchangeable, would there be any craving for sentence meanings? Obviously not. We would know enough about something if we knew whether or not it was a sentence; knowing anything else about it would not help us any further. Thus the whole point of knowing the meaning of a sentence boils down to knowing what there is about the sentence that prohibits it from being interchangeable with other sentences. That is, we want to know what a sentence means because we want to know why uttering it is saying something different from what is said by uttering another sentence. Accounting for sentence meanings amounts to accounting for why uttering different sentences results in different utterance meanings. Reformulating this, we may say: Sentence meanings are what have to be attributed to sentences in order to account for why they differ in serviceability for producing utterance meanings.

Now this is exactly what our *sms* are. We had to attribute them to NIVEAU's signs because we saw no better way of accounting for how these signs differ in their serviceability for producing utterance meanings. This, then, is why I regard our *sms* as paradigmatic sentence meanings: as theoretical entities which *have to be attributed* to signs which are sufficient for making meaningful utterances (given suitable circumstances), if *we want to* establish a theory which accounts for how people can say things by using these signs.

§ 40 Sentence meaning defined

If, for one more section, we can forget about the difference between sentences which are syntactically structured and unstructured signs which can also be used to make utterances, then through the preceding considerations I hope to have made a good case for the idea that if the sentences of a language have been specified, sentence meanings are theoretical features that have to be attributed to the sentences in order to provide for the empirical correctness and completeness of rules which specify meanings of utterances in this language. Therefore, attributions of sentence meanings to whole sentences are good in the same measure as they are part of a good theory of utterance meaning. The following definitons are intended to express this idea:

Let $\Gamma$ be a language[102] such that the utterance meaning of using $\sigma$ in $s$ is $\Gamma(\sigma, s)$. Let $S$ define $S(\sigma)$[103] for all $\sigma$ of $\Gamma$. Let $P$ define $P(S(\sigma), s)$ such that for all $\sigma$ and $s$, $P(S(\sigma), s) = \Gamma(\sigma, s)$. Then

(Def. 1) $\sigma$ has sentence meaning *sm* in $\Gamma$ iff

(1)  $P, S$ is the best description of $\Gamma$, and

(2)  $S(\sigma) = sm$.

'*S*' is intended to suggest semantics (and '*sm*' is to suggest 'sentence meaning', of course), '*P*' to suggest pragmatics. The distinctions $S$ draws between signs are to be regarded as conjectures about differences between signs which are a plausible relative to the rules for utterance meanings

---

102) See § 24.

103) '$S(\sigma, s)$' for ambiguous sentences.

specified by *P*. If a different *P'* were tried, other differences between the signs would have to be postulated by some *S'*, and since *P'*, *S'* might come out empirically correct and complete too, its distinctions between the signs would be different conjectures about differences between the signs. Thus the differences between the signs, and any features used to mark the differences, are plausibly postulated relative to the set of rules for utterance meanings which they are supposed to launch. This point is made more explicit by (Def. 2):

...(Def. 2) a sentence $\sigma$ has the sentence meaning *sm* relative to *P* in $\Gamma$ iff

(1)  *P*, *S* is a better description of $\Gamma$ than any other *P*, *S'*, and
(2)  $S(\sigma) = sm$.

While (Def. 2) takes *P* to be given and *S* to be its best supplement, (Def. 1) requires that *P*, *S* be a better description of $\Gamma$ than any other *P'*, *S'*.

In order to speak of *the* meaning of a given sentence in an absolute sense, we have to require that there be a singular assignment; this requirement is included in (Def. 1) by referring to assignments within the best description of the language in question. There may be different constraints on 'best' descriptions, corresponding to partially different concepts of sentence meaning. All the same, the best description may not exist. In this case, some sentences may lack sentence meanings in an absolute sense.

## § 41 Two different tasks in the study of sentence meaning

Let me now try to defend my attempt at claiming to establish insights into the status of sentence meaning, but all the while crouching at a niveau far below the level of structured sentences. Did I not just claim to say something on semantics? And is not semantics the study of how the meanings of sentences result from the meanings of their parts? How, then, could there be a semantics for a language whose so—called 'sentences' have no parts at all?

There seem to be at least two quite different tasks involved in explicating the concept of sentence meaning in natural languages. The first is to do semantics proper, i.e. to show either generally or for a particular language how the meaning of a sentence results from the meanings of its parts. The second is to do something different, viz. to show either generally or for a particular language how the use of a whole sentence with a given meaning contributes to the meaning of an utterance of this sentence. Performing the second task amounts to a justification of the claim that the things defined as sentence meanings by a semantics are "meanings" in an interesting sense of the word. The second task has been executed in different ways, partly bold, partly painstaking, partly even both: For instance, by giving a definition of sentence meaning in terms of utterance meaning in the manner of W.P. Alston,[104] or by describing how a theory might look which was to describe a community's language in an empirically testable way in the manner of D. Lewis or of S. Schiffer,[105] or by specifiying a method of investigating linguistic behavior and arriving at confirmed hypotheses about meanings of sentences and words in the manner of J. Bennett.[106]

Whereas these philosophers also took part in the research program concerned with the first task, the present chapter is only another step in completing the second. My definition of sentence meaning does not do the job of a semantics; it states what a semantics must achieve in order to supply definitions of sentence meanings. It is by no means a trivial task to show that something is a sentence meaning. Imagine an ambitious linguist (or philosopher) coming up with a general semantics for languages in some canonical orthographic form:

> The meaning of a word is the number of its letters; the meaning of a sentence is the sum of the meanings of its component words.

Despite the obvious simplicity and elegance of his definition, the linguist fails to win our approval. However, if we tell him that we are not prepared to accept length for meaning we ought to give him reasons. On the other hand, if some linguist or philosopher offers the truth conditions of sentences as their meanings, he has to give us reasons as well. What way is there to argue for classifying a given type of entities as sentence meanings?

The object of the present section is to canvass for a certain way of establishing that entities described as sentence meanings by a semantics really are sentence meanings. Put in other word: In so much as the object of a semantics is to specify sentence meanings I am canvassing for a certain way of assessing a semantics. On the other hand, I will say nothing about what such a semantics might look like. But is it really possible to distinguish both tasks?

I definitely think so. To illustrate this point, let me compare the study of sentence meanings with the study of vacuum cleaners. If I am offered some object as a vacuum cleaner, I may try out whether the object really

---

104) W.P. Alston, *Philosophy of Language*, p. 36.
105) See D. Lewis, *Convention*, ch. 5, and S. Schiffer, *Meaning*, ch. VI.
106) The aim of his *Linguistic Behaviour*.

is a vacuum cleaner by investigating what it achieves: It must be suitable for removing dust and dirt and the like, and it must achieve this by sucking in air and by somehow collecting the dust, dirt, etc, inside. Investigating this, however, is not a very thoroughgoing investigation; there may be more informative answers, an interesting general one and some interesting special ones. The interesting general answer says that in all the interesting cases, a vacuum cleaner has an electric motor (electricity being the only energy avialable in normal apartments) on whose armature shaft a ventilator is fixed (because any indirect connection would be too susceptible to breakdown) which sucks in air through a dust bag ( not just a dust filter, because only dust bags permit sufficiently long cleaning time). Interesting special answers may tell us that vacuum cleaners (floor model) are more efficient than upright vacuum cleaners, or that some vacuum cleaners require disposable vacuum bags to be inserted in their dust bags, or that the power of vacuum cleaners with side — air valves can be regulated.

Now the question as to what something must achieve in order to be a vacuum cleaner parallels my question as to what something must achieve in order to be a sentence meaning. The interesting general answer is to parallel general semantics: Given certain general features of a language — for instance quantification, sentence embedding, indefinite length of sentences —, its sentence meanings will be structured in certain general ways. And the interesting special answers are intended to parallel the semantics of natural languages which share the general features; they will then tell us in which manners the general semantic structures are realized in these languages.

The point of our comparison is simply this: I can check out whether something is a vacuum cleaner *without any knowledge*, general or special, as to how any vacuum cleaner is constructed; and it is necessary that I can check this out *in all my ignorance*, if general or special theories on how to build vacuum cleaners are to be testable. In just the same way, it is necessary that I can check out whether something is the meaning of some sentence independently of any information about its structure, if general or special semantics are to be testable; and luckily I can in fact check this out without any information about that something's structure.

Using NIVEAU's unstructured signs as examples for a procedure by which structured sentences are tested for sentence meanings means nothing but *abstracting from* structural information in applying such a procedure — all the while being fully aware that the sentences might have a structure which is relevant for their having their meanings.[107] This procedure would not have to be changed if a good nose discovered structure in NIVEAU's signs. I would be surprised; but the *sms* of the wholes would remain unaltered even if they were discovered to be composed of smaller *wms* ("word meanings"). Of course, the theoretical fruitfulness of attributing *sms* to signs would be enormously increased in such a case. For we would then be able to actually predict the *sms* of new signs over and above new driving maneuver signs.

## § 42 The theoretical character of sentence meaning

In order to illustrate the theoretical character of sentence meaning let me make two comparisons. The first one is more natural for someone who is impressed by the singular status of speakers' utterances. The second one might be more appealing to someone who considers what a complicated task it is to find out which circumstance in the whole utterance situation can be regarded as the speaker's utterance. The first comparison is intended to stress the idea that sentence meaning is explanatory with regard to and thus a great deal more theoretical than utterance meaning (which is itself a theoretical entity). The second comparison assimilates the forces of utterance situation features to the meanings of sentences; it hints at regarding the stock of linguistic devices as consisting of two parts, one more manipulable than the other.

If we are very impressed by speakers' utterances, then we shall quickly discover many signs of NIVEAU. Now if we were blind to all differences between utterance meanings which result from using different signs, we should treat all signs alike and, in the ways sketched in chapter III, should discover that they are used in making utterances and that these utterances have certain menaings according to rules which we hypothetically assume to be valid. So far this wouldn't differ from what we have done with NIVEAU zero. The essential thing has been to postulate utterance meanings by assuming utterance meaning rules to be valid. These assumptions are justified by inference to the best explanation

---

107) B. Loar has used the same point in an argument against Davidsonian semantics: If a theory uses facts about the structures of sentences for deriving their truth conditions, it will not *thereby* avoid accidental equivalences ('Snow is white' is true iff grass is green) which are irrelevant with respect to meaning. For there are signs which lack structure but mean the same as some sentences; in their case, structure will not be helpful. ('Two Theories of Meaning', pp. 144f.)

of perturbations in the conventional system of the group under consideration. Confirmation depended essentially on finding utterance candidates in every case.

Recall Neptune from § 25: Adams and Leverrier had theoretically postulated Neptune's mass and orbit, because postulating a planet with this mass and this orbit was the best explanation for perturbations in Uranus' proper orbit. Confirmation of this explanation depended essentially on finding a silvery speck where Neptune was to be located if the hypothetical, explanatory orbit were correct.

Now, for the sake of our comparison, let us *forget* all of the following: After its discovery, Neptune became a planet which was as familiar as any planet could desire to be. It was observed repeatedly, and its orbit was not only theoretically postulated, it was observationally controlled — with the implication that its mass was not just as postulated as before: it was simply known. However, Neptune's orbit turned out to be distorted,[108] just as was formerly the case with Uranus' orbit. Even after the discovery of Neptune and its influence, the now refined description of Uranus' orbit still did not fit in with observational data. As in the Uranus case the same suspicion occurred to astronomers; and independently from one another, Percival Lowell (in 1915) and William Henry Pickering (in 1919) both calculated the mass and orbit of this unknown planet, going on the assumption that one unknown planet was responsible for the perturbations. If this assumption as well as their calculations were correct, then in 1930 'Transneptune' would be expected in a certain region of the sky. This region was photographed twice by Clyde William Tombaugh; and he found that a suitable speck had moved.

Let us forget these historical facts and invent a new story. Imagine that Neptune had never been observed (due to insufficient telescopes). He would, therefore, have enjoyed the continued existence of a theoretical entity, although a well—confirmed one, because its influence on Uranus' deviation, which was to be predicted from its postulated position, would have been there. Indulging in further fantasies, however, let us imagine newly discovered deviations — perturbations too small to be discovered by once—used instruments. Some astronomers begin to doubt the existence of Neptune; traditionalists (who are planet lovers) take a different route. "Of course", they say, "if unobserved Neptune is as we assume it to be, and if it travels in the orbit we suppose it to travel in, then Uranus' newly discovered extravagancies are unexplainable. But

---

108) Third hand astronomy again, from *Encyclopaedia Britannica*, 1971, s.v. Pluto.

suppose that our unobserved Neptune is distracted from its well-defined orbit by another planet which is even farther out? What would this planet's mass and orbit have to look like in order to account for those perturbations in (unobserved) Neptune's orbit which would account for the observed, but still unexplained perturbations in Uranus' deviations?" After solving some complicated mathematical problems, our astronomers come up with the mass and orbit of an unobserved planet (which they call 'Pluto') which very well explain unobserved perturbations in (unobserved) Neptune's orbit. These in turn explain observed perturbations in Uranus' deviations from its proper orbit. – Here my fantastic story comes to an end.

From our background conventions (Uranus' proper orbit) there were deviations; we explained these by positing utterance meanings (Neptune's mass and orbit) of one way of signalling. Then there were differences in utterance meanings (perturbations in posited Neptune's orbit); these we explained by positing further entities, viz. sentence meanings (Pluto's mass and orbit).

In this picture, sentence meanings are theoretical entities which we have to posit because otherwise we cannot account for differences in other theoretical entities, viz. utterance meanings. I find this picture persuasive if we think of language as having developed from one way of signalling (or from several interchangeable ways of signalling). If we imagine that from the start language developed from the use of different signals – as iconicity theories of origin would suggest –, our second comparison might seem more instructive:

There are diffferent circumstances which together effect a deviation from a conventional situation which is determined by background conventions. For example, there are circumstances like salient interests; behavioral patterns like slowing down; and the particular behavioral pattern of using things which (from the point of view of a language imputing description) are to be described as signs. Some of these circumstances are completely or almost completely uncontrollable by the people who are involved. On the other hand, they have their behavioral patterns at their disposal. Now the greater the communicative efficiency of a language, the better its chances are to survive together with the group which uses it; and communicative efficiency is increased with the number of possible utterance meanings. This number is increased if more behavioral patterns differ in their influence on the conventional situation. Thus there is an evolutionary pressure on languages to develop more and more behavioral patterns which differ with respect to their serviceability for producing utterance meanings. We may say that there will be an evolutionary pressure to develop more and more behavioral patterns which differ in meaning ('meaning' meaning 'sentence meaning' rather than 'utterance meaning'). The evolutionary function of developing meanings of behavioral patterns consists in making more utterance meanings possible.

Some behavioral patterns are more easily manipulable than others; some are cheaper; some are more modifiable. The evolution of meanings will concentrate on such behavioral patterns — the prominent way in which languages become more efficient, then, consists in the treatment of more and more signs by group members as different in meaning. Sentence meanings, therefore, may be viewed as a special class of behavioral pattern meanings.

*Warning*: Behavioral patterns have been assimilated to signs. In this context, there are two possible parallels. Either we compare *utterances of* sentences (*instances of using* signs) with *performances of* behavioral patterns, abstracting in both cases from all other features of the situation. Or, we compare *sentences* (*signs*) (which then are things to be uttered or used) with *behavioral patterns* (which then are things to be performed). Sentences and signs have sentence meanings (sign meanings); if behavioral patterns have meanings, their meanings have the same theoretical status as do sentence meanings. If a sentence is uttered, its meaning contributes to the utterance meaning — provided that the sentence is uttered in a situation where the utterance in fact has an utterance meaning. (If I am alone in my study and utter 'Go!', then I have uttered a meaningful sentence. However, I have not made a meaningful utterance.) If a meaningful behavioral pattern is performed, its meaning contributes to the utterance meaning — provided that the behavioral pattern is performed in a situation where there is an uttterance which in fact has an utterance meaning. (If I slow down, then I have performed a meaningful driving maneuver; however, if no driver is present who could make use of my slowing down then even if I flash my beams, I have not made a meaningful utterance.)

Sentences and utterances are often distinguished by calling them 'sentence types' and 'sentence tokens'. This is misleading, for it favors the impression that utterances of meaningful sentences are *ipso facto* meaningful utterances. Meaningful utterances of sentences are tokens of meaningful utterance types only because they are instances of situations characterized by some features which are relevant for the utterance meaning — among them the feature that "a sentence token is present" (that "a sentence is uttered").

## § 43 Sentence meaning is conceptually irreducible

The theoretical status of sentence meanings might be further clarified by showing that there are some things which they cannot be reduced to − provided only that these things can be viewed as appealing reduction bases which are in some obvious sense less theoretical than are sentence meanings. I shall discuss four reductive attempts insofar as these are intended to be plausible on intuitive grounds, i.e. more or less *a priori*.

*Illocutionary act potential*: Utterance meaning is less theoretical than is sentence meaning; and it is an interesting reduction bases because an influential and attractive doctrine of linguistic meaning aims at such a reduction, namely the doctrine that meaning is use. To be sure, this doctrine would also reduce utterance meaning to something still more tangible, viz. to the role which an utterance plays in a language game. However, here I am only concerned with the first mentioned step.

Before showing that it is not possible to reduce sentence meaning to utterance meaning, let me stress that I adhere to the doctrine that meaning is use. The present book is simply a defense of this doctrine. For, as defended by Wittgenstein, its leading idea would have it that languages are not accidentally used by groups whose members follow social rules; rather, linguistic behavior is a special kind of rule−guided behavior. It is for conceptual reasons that languages are embedded in rule−guided behavior; or as I prefer to put it (for the mere reason that I like the picture), languages exist where conventional systems are impregnated with language, i.e. where conventional systems have a particular, complex superstructure.

Speaking loosely, then, we might feel tempted to say that languages are nothing but a complex structure within conventional behavior. Ought not therefore meanings, and sentence meanings in particular, be nothing but identifiable elements in conventional behavior? (Possibly very complex elements, if necessary.) Although one has a sense about what this idea is aiming at, it is difficult to cast it in a form which is precise enough to be discussed. The most clear−cut reduction of sentence meaning to sentence use which at the same time is a reduction of sentence meaning to utterance meaning is due to William P. Alston.[109]

---

109) See p.117, fn.104. D.E. Cooper ('Meaning and Illocutions') has convincingly argued against D. Holdcroft ('Meaning and Illocutionary Acts') and L.J. Cohen ('Do Illocutionary Forces Exist?') that even if identified with illocutionary act potential, sentence meaning can and ought to be distinguished from the illocutionary acts (and aspects thereof) which are performed in uttering sentences. Alston's reduction is thus

I am using this reduction as a paradigm in order to show how the doctrine that meaning is use must not be overstated. The discussion about whether meaning is use is more indebted to Alston's definitional courage that is manifested by the disregard for his definition which prevails in the literature.

Alston's idea is stated in terms of the 'illocutionary act potential' of a sentence, which I will henceforth call its 'iap'. The iap of a sentence comprises the illocutionary acts which can be performed by uttering it. Now as Holdcroft has pointed out,[110] the concept of an iap is open to different interpretations. The alternative mentioned by Holdcroft is this: Either an iap comprises only illocutionary forces (like warning, requesting, and the like), or it comprises what we would call utterance meanings, i.e. pairs of illocutionary forces and propositions (like informing that it is raining, requesting that you come, requesting that you go, and the like). The iaps of two sentences might coincide in the former sense but differ in the latter, as with 'It is snowing', 'It is raining', or with 'Come!' and 'Go!'. A second alternative for interpreting the concept of an iap, which Holdcroft did not consider, is whether the iap of a sentence is a class of utterance meanings (or illocutionary forces), or a function from utterance situations into utterance meanings (or illocutionary forces). That is to say: Either we consider what we can do with a sentence in any circumstances whatsoever, then collect all these linguistic acts in a class, and finally call this class the sentence's iap. Or we consider pairs of situations and linguistic acts, such that each situation in which the sentence can be used is paired off with the linguistic act performed by using it in this situation; these pairs are collected to form the sentence's iap (which will then be a function as described above). 'Come!' and 'Go!' may both be requests and recommendations, though only in different situations. This difference will not result in making both iap's different if they are classes of illocutionary forces. However, if their iaps are functions from situations into illocutionary forces, they will differ. 'It is snowing' and 'It is raining' may both be recommendations to go out, though in different circumstances. If their iaps are classes of utterance meanings, this fact cannot make them different; however, if they are functions from situations into utterance meanings, they will differ. As the examples show, if Alston's thesis is to have a fair trial,

---

Continued:
shown to lack the unwelcome consequence that sentence meaning cannot be kept distinct from utterance meaning. However, the reduction will be shown to have another undesirable consequence.

110) 'Meaning an Illocutionary Acts', sect. 2.

'illocutionary act potential' must be construed in the most discriminating sense.[111] Therefore, I take a sentence's iap to be the function which takes as arguments the situations where it can be used to say something and whose values are the utterance meanings produced by using it.

Now Alston straightforwardly identified the meaning of a sentence with this sentence's illocutionary act potential. Why should this be true? Consider: If two signs have one and the same iap, then nobody, in any situation, can use one sign to say something which differs from what he would say were he to use the other sign instead. Therefore, both signs do not differ in their serviceability to produce utterance meanings; thus they do not differ in meaning. Their meanings are identical. (And of course, if their meanings are identical, then their iaps are too.) But if identity of iap means identity of sentence meaning, then why distinguish between iap and sentence meaning? There can be no point to such a distinction. (And of course, if sentence meaning is identical with iap, then identiy of iap is the same as identity of sentence meaning.) Therefore, that sentence meaning is illocutionary act potential goes with the fact that sentence synonymity goes with iap — identity.

Now whereas from the synonymity of two sentences of some language it follows that both have the same iap in this language, the pragmatics being sensitive only to sentence meaning differences, the converse does not hold. The fact that two sentences of a language have the same iap in this language must not entail that both are synonymous in this language in the sense of being effectively attributed one and the same sentence meaning by the language's semantics. For no sentence meaning — be it a 'that' — clause or a set of truth conditions — must be used up for the description of one language; maybe it will be needed for the description of a further language, too. This follows immediately from the possibility of correct sentence translation; but even a philosopher who, in spite of established philological practice, is bold enough to doubt this possibility cannot rule out that, by shere accident, the best description of English might ascribe to one English sentence exactly the same meaning as the best description of German ascribes to some German sentence.

There may even be two sentences in English which are translatable into German sentences, and this might happen to English sentences which have the same illocutionary act potential whereas their German counterparts don't — just because the pragmatics of German and English are different. This empirical possibility would be ruled out in advance if from the illocutionary act potential identity of our two English sentences

---

111) This point was developed in discussions with Irene Heim.

we could infer their synonymity: since each of them has the same meaning as one of the two German sentences, these would be synonymous, too. We would be forced to handle German speakers' differences in dealing with both of them by reshaping our − best! − assumptions on German background conventions in order to arrive at utterance meaning rules which give us identical illocutionary act potentials.[112]

To express matters realistically: If sentence meanings are accepted as entities which are theoretically fruitful in describing the use of a language, then they can be rediscovered in other languages. There, they can explain facts different from what they explain in the first language.

*Speakers' meanings' core*: At least two prominent philosophers apparently use the thrust of speaker's/s' meaning to leap over to sentence meaning, viz. Schiffer and Bennett. This is courageous because there is a problem lurking in the depths. Let us grant that what a speaker means determines in one way or other what his utterance means. But then what he means will determine, not how he means his sentence, but what he means *by uttering* this sentence. Thus even if meaning $x$ by uttering $\sigma$ somehow results in the meaning of an *utterance* of $\sigma$ being $x$, it will not result with equal plausibility in the meaning of $\sigma$ being $x$. For whereas the utterance of $\sigma$ was somehow meant, $\sigma$ itself was not.

This problem would be easily solved if speakers meant the same thing with every utterance of $\sigma$. For the sentence meaning of $\sigma$ might then be defined as what is meant by all utterances of $\sigma$. This is precisely Bennett's way:

> "I shall use the form '$S$ means $P$' as shorthand for 'There is a non−coincidental regularity such that whenever a tribesman utters a token of type $S$ he means by it that $P$'." (*Linguistic Behaviour*, p. 213)

"$S$" are what I call signs, i.e. those behavioral features of the utterance situation the performance of which means using a sign, or uttering a sentence. The description of such an $S$ does not include any further features of the utterance situation. The "$P$"s are sentence meanings; they

---

112) The point seems to be generalizable: Any definition of the meaning of an expression in terms of a reductive function (e.g. from possible worlds onto truth values, or from contexts into contents) amounts to a restriction on semantic descriptions which effectively give meanings in such a way that meanings of two expressions from different languages can be identical. For instance, if linguists had good independent reasons to assume identical meanings for 'I' and 'ich', then a definition of this type would force them to handle any pragmatic difference below the stipulated reduction level. The empirical import of such a restriction is not predictable.

are listed in what Bennett calls a "sentence dictionary" (*ibid.*), composed of entities like '*S* means *P*'.

Whether this move is successful depends, of course, on whether the required regularities are likely to exist. There will be "scattered exceptions" (*ibid.*) — one might think of performance mistakes. Furthermore, there may be ambiguous sentences; Bennett excludes consideration of ambiguity from this context. Finally, he allows two *P*s to be identical if both differ only in indexical features (p. 216). But will this procedure of composing sentence dictionaries be successful for perfect speakers of languages in which there is no ambiguity? *Only if utterance meanings are completely independent of the utterance situation.* (Except for indexicality.) The straightforward identification of sentence meaning with what is (always or conventionally) meant by uttering a sentence is only possible if what is meant depends only on the sentence which is uttered.[113]

I think that at this point Bennett overlooks a vital difference between utterance meaning and sentence meaning. (Recall our way of establishing a sentence dictionary in Bennett's sense, viz. the semantics of NIVEAU. We could never have completed this by looking for speakers who always say the same things by using certain signs.) There may perhaps be languages in which the sentence meanings completely determine the utterance meanings of the sentences, and vice versa. However, this cannot be stipulated in advance; we must be prepared to encounter languages like NIVEAU, or English, where the connection is less direct.

Neither Schiffer nor Bennett have claimed that in order for sentences to be meaningful, speakers must mean them. They sort of replaced 'meaning a sentence' with 'meaning always the same by uttering a sentence'. Once again, this is an expression of the idea that 'meaning is where something is meant'. But they did not carry this principle so far as to invoke it for the meaningfulness of sub—sentential linguistic elements. Once we are convinced that for an expression to be meaningful it is sufficient for it to contribute to the meaning of something else, we may be sure that word meanings will be entities which we have to attribute to words because we cannot otherwise account for sentences having their meanings (which we have to attribute to them because we cannot otherwise account for utterances having their meanings). And just as we cannot (and need not!) account for the meaning of a sentence by

---

113) In the context of this discussion, we have of course to disregard quarrels about the connection between what is meant, or conventionally meant, and utterance meaning. — Schiffer makes the same move as Bennett (see *Meaning*, pp. 119—128); Bennett's proposal is easier to compare with our case study.

mistakenly claiming that speakers always mean the same by uttering it, so it is needless and will presumably be mistaken to claim, in order to account for a word's meaning, that speakers always mean the same by uttering this word.

*Constant proposition of utterance meanings*: Sentence meaning is not even close enough to utterance meaning to play a certain role which can be characterized by the following principle:

> Let $\sigma$ be a sentence whose disambiguated and de – indexicalized meaning can be rendered by a 'that' – clause; then precisely the same 'that' – clause can be used to render the proposition of the meaning of any literal utterance made in using $\sigma$.

I cannot cite anyone to have explicitly subscribed to this principle. But there is plenty of evidence that it is part of contemporary philosophical background knowledge – at least where speech act theory is taken seriously. One piece of evidence is the usual way of expounding speech act theory: If the linguistic meaning of a sentence is clear and if its sense and reference are determined (i.e. if there is no further question arising from ambiguity or indexicality), then the proposition of what has been said in using the sentence on any occasion can be reported by a 'that' – clause which simply embeds this very same sentence, regardless of the varying illocutionary forces.[114] Another piece of evidence is the theory of indirect speech acts which treats every utterance of an indicative sentence $S$ in a non – question – asking tone of voice as literally having the meaning of an asserion that $S$, even if the "direct" conventional force is quite different. A third piece of evidence comes from contemporary philosophy of language's preoccupation with assertive utterances of indicative sentences for which the principle is most plausible.

Prima facie, the theory of literalness proposed by Bach and Harnish could be used as a statement of the principle.[115] The linguistic meaning of the expression the speaker utters (e.g. "Are you going to leave?") is disambiguated ("Are you going to resign?") and provided with a reference ("Are you, Friedrich Zimmermann, going to resign?"). What

---

114) See, e.g., J.L. Austin, *How to Do Things with Words*, Lecture VIII; the 'that' – clause renders his 'rheme'. Austin's locutionary act is an aspect of *utterance* meaning! See further J. Searle, *Speech Acts*, 2.1 and 2.4; his extremely strong condition 9 (in the analysis of promising in 3.1., p. 61) to the effect that the sentence meaning determines both illocutionary force and proposition of the utterance meaning is weakened on p. 68 only to the extent that the illocutionary force may be supplied by the utterance situation.

115) *Linguistic Communication and Speech Acts*, pp. 9 – 11, 60 – 81.

results is split up into a force operator (corresponding to the syntactic form) and a proposition, and this is the locutionary act which is the literal *utterance* meaning: a question whether Friedrich Zimmermann is going to resign. The utterance is a literal illocutionary act if it is an illocutionary act with the propositional content that Friedrich Zimmermann is going to resign and with a force which, in a sense to be explained, is compatible with a question.

This theory does not, however, admit comparison with the present approach because Bach and Harnish use it within the framework of a theory of communication which starts from the idea[116] that someone who hears a speaker utter an expression infers, from his knowledge of this expression's linguistic meaning, and aided by mutual contextual beliefs and shared general assumptions, what the speaker's communicative intent is. At one step in this chain of inferences, the hearer arrives at a conclusion which is labelled his 'belief about the locutionary act'. If we waive the misleading picture of rapid and unconscious inferences, we may understand Bach and Harnish to posit an information processing program such that at some intermediary stage the hearer is in a state which he would have arrived at earlier if the speaker, instead of uttering "Are you going to leave?" had uttered: "I ask whether Friedrich Zimmermann is going to resign." I do not think that it is very helpful to project this hypothesis about how hearers' brains work, on facts about utterance meanings. But be that as it may — such facts would have nothing to do with conventional meaning in the sense of the present aproach.

The above principle expresses the idea that all the situation contributes to the utterance meaning is filling in indexical gaps, disambiguating, and adding the illocutionary force, while the proposition is provided by the sentence — it is the sentence's meaning. Going on the assumption that the numbers both of sentences and of illocutionary forces are finite for a language, the principle implies that there is only a finite number of utterance meanings in this language (apart from indexicality).

It is immediately clear that although most of NIVEAU's signs have sentence meanings that can be rendered by 'that'—clauses, the 'that'—clauses rendering the propositions of the meanings of utterances which are made in using the signs may be quite different.[117] And all such uses

---

116) *L.c.*, pp. 91—93.
117) Robert C. Stalnaker, in 'Asserting', has argued a related point: "What one says — the proposition he expresses — is itself something that might have been different if the facts had been different; ..." (p. 317). Therefore, for him a sentence does not

of signs are literal in the sense of being neither metaphorical nor ironical nor anything like this. (For instance, if a truck driver uses his left blinker to inform a driver who follows him that he may not pass him he is by no means lying ("I want to turn left") for a morally good purpose.) The ways in which sentence meanings contribute to the propositions of utterance meanings depend upon the utterance meaning rules.

Take the sentence 'The dog bites'. According to the utterance situation, the speaker may recommend (as a dog — breeder) that the customer buy the dog, advise (as a burglar) that his fellow burglar better choose a different house, warn (as a dog — owner) the visitor not to approach the dog, etc., etc. There is no question that the sentence 'The dog bites' means that the dog bites. However, there is no reason at all why there should be a 'basic' (and pretty well hidden) *utterance* meaning in every case where the sentence is used — something like that the speaker asserts that the dog bites — from which the addressee intelligently infers what the speaker is up to. The plain fact is that there are more ways of determining an utterance meaning's proposition than identifying it with the uttered sentence's disambiguated and de — indexicalized meaning.

*Truth conditions*: The idea that the meaning of a sentence consists in its truth conditions is straightforward: We know the meaning of a sentence if and only if we know under which circumstances it would be true. If I stick to my definition of sentence meaning, then it is, of course, an open question whether truth conditions will do the required job. The identity of sentence meaning with a sentence's truth conditions becomes an empirical question which has to be asked anew for every newly discovered language. I shall ask the question for NIVEAU. The answer will be negative: If my description of NIVEAU is the best one (which I am sure it is not), then sentence meanings are not in general identical with truth conditions. As is clear from this way of discussing it, I am only criticizing the *a priori* version of the truth condition theory of meaning which tries to establish the identiy of sentence meaning and truth conditions by the sole premise of a sentence's intelligibility or testability. I cannot, of course, argue from NIVEAU that the truth conditions of

---

Continued:

determine what is said (a proposition) but rather a propositional concept, i.e. a function from possible worlds into propositions (p. 318). The interesting question, of course, is what this function precisely looks like. Investigating it in the context of constative uses of indicative sentences of English — as Stalnaker does — is obviously more difficult than investigating the utterance meaning rules of NIVEAU.

English sentences cannot, for empirical reasons, be profitably regarded as their meanings in the sense of my definition.

Before showing what I have promised to show, I have to solve two problems in interpreting the theory I am criticizing.

The first problem results from the necessary fairness which advises us to restrict the scope of the theory to declarative sentences. This is a syntactical notion, which is not easily transferable from one language to another. I think we should interpret it with a mixture of semantical and epistemological elements: A sentence should be counted as declarative if it is identical in sentence meaning with an English declarative sentence which, in turn, has a cognitive content (cognitive beyond any reasonable doubt). The reasons for this interpretation are hopefully obvious. The theory will then concern all signs of NIVEAU to which we had to attribute *sm*s which are designated by 'that' – clauses; all of these signs have the same meaning as the English sentence which follows the 'that', and all of these sentences are straightforwardly empirical.

The second problem results from calling sentences true or false. What is meant is usually quite a different thing. Take a declarative English sentence, $\sigma$, which means that $p$. It will then be possible to use $\sigma$, under a great variety of circumstances, to make constative utterances whose utterance meanings contain the proposition that $p$. For instance, by uttering 'It is raining' (whose meaning I take to be that it is raining) we can state, inform, guess, claim, argue, predict, report (and so forth) that it is raining. Now all of these utterances may be, or may come out true or false. Such uses of these sentences are even standard in 'stationary' contexts like newscasts, newspapers, and books. This is why one tends to ignore differences between statements, claims, reports, etc., on the one hand, and those sentences which are especially suitable for being uttered in stating, claiming, reporting, etc., on the other.

I think that a philosopher who accepts the fundamental idea of the theory that the meaning of a (declarative) sentence consists in its truth conditions, but who dislikes speaking of sentences as true or false, might well express the theory in the following way:

> The truth condition of any constative utterance which is made in using a declarative sentence which means that $p$, is that $p$.

For instance: the truth condition of any statement, claim, report, ..., which is made in using the sentence 'It is raining' (which means that it is raining), is that it is raining.

If we take both interpretative steps − i.e. if we interpret 'declarative' as 'having as meaning a cognitive $p$' and if we interpret 'truth conditions of $\sigma$' as 'truth conditions of every constative utterance of $\sigma$' − , then, if applied to NIVEAU, the theory says the following:

(A) Every constative utterance which is made by using a sign with a 'that $p$' − $sm$ is an information [118] that $p$.

(B) If every constative utterance which is made by using $\sigma$ ($\sigma$ being serviceable for constative utterances)[119] is an information that $p$, then $\sigma$ means that $p$.

Both (A) and (B) are wrong for NIVEAU. This can easily be seen for (A): (A) is true for constative utterances resulting from uses of rule (17.2), but it is wrong because rule (16)[120] permits speakers to use signs which mean that $p$ in order to inform addressees of facts other than $p$. Since the truth conditions of the information may differ from $p$ (e.g. the truth conditions of '$A$ does $V$' differ from '$A$ may do $V$'), the meaning of the sign does not determine the truth conditions of the utterances.

Against (B), there is only a weak counterexample in NIVEAU which I shall not elaborate upon. (It isn't that interesting, after all.) Let me just note that is is an empirical question whether or not a counterexample exists. If it does, then (B) is empirically incorrect, provided my definition of sentence meaning is accepted. Therefore, (B) cannot be held to be true on intuitive grounds.

Taking for granted that the meaning of a sentence $\sigma$ is what we have to attribute to it in order to account for the meanings of *all* of its utterances, we cannot fail to see that for declarative sentences, this meaning need not determine circumstances which would make all *constative* utterances of $\sigma$ true. Therefore, without the aid of further knowledge of utterance meaning rules, knowing the meaning of a declarative sentence does not imply that one knows under which conditions constative utterances of the sentence are true. The reason for this, of course, is very closely related to what we observed above: The meaning of a sentence does not uniquely determine the proposition of the meanings of utterances of this sentence. If (B) is false too, then knowing the conditions under which constative utterances of a declarative sentence $\sigma$ are true is not sufficient for knowing the meaning of $\sigma$.

---

118) This is the only kind of constative utterance in NIVEAU.

119) This condition is to exclude, as trivial counterexamples, driving maneuvers, which cannot be used for constative utterances in NIVEAU.

120) See Appendix II for both rules.

# Epilogue

## § Rules of language

This final section will not attempt to add anything of systematical interest. Its modest aim is to use results we have hopefully achieved, in contributing to the clarification of the concept of a rule of language, or a linguistic rule. This concept, as well as related ones, have played and still play a mostly helpful role in philosophical discussions. Its role could possibly be even healthier still if some ambiguities were avoided more often then they are in fact avoided. Avoiding ambiguities becomes easier if one realizes systematic connections between different interpretations. Therefore, what I shall try to do is to sketch systematic connections between different things which may be called 'rules of language'.

I shall not pronounce preferences about which of these different things best deserves the label in question. For as we shall see, in the very concept of rules of language, there is an unresolvable tension between rules, on the one hand, and language, on the other. At their best, rules directly and immediately prescribe well — defined kinds of bahavior. Language, at its best, is a theoretical and abstract superstructure of extremely complex systems of rule — guided behavior. The more a statement tells us about a given language, the more diffuse its information is about the rules which guide the behavior of the group which uses this language. The more concrete information is about what members of a group accept each other as doing or omitting, the more is left open about the language they are using.

Let me proceed by using a simple example, viz. the sentence 'Pass me the salt, please'. There are syntactic rules which tell us why this string of phonemes is an English sentence. I shall remain silent about syntactic rules because I have not dealt with them. There is only one thing which we have encountered which might be called a rule of English at this level:

'Pass me the salt, please' is an English sentence.

This means that there is at least one situation where uttering this string of phonemes has an utterance meaning according to some other rules of English which we shall coome across presently.

Now 'Pass me the salt, please' has not only a syntactic structure, but also a semantic composition. Again, I shall remain silent, for the reason given above. The only kind of rule at this level which I have dealt with is something like the following. (*My example is certainly wrong*; it is just modelled after similar signs in NIVEAU.)

'Pass me the salt, please' has the sentence meaning that the addressee passes the speaker the salt.

This is a linguistic rule on the semantic level. Other rules of this type state, for instance, synonymity or entailment relations between sentences.

The next kind of linguistic rules is something like the following: (Again, *the example is wrong*, I'm sure.)

If the speaker is standardly interested in the addressee's passing him the salt and if the addressee is normally able to pass it, then if the speaker utters a sentence with the sentence meaning that the addressee passes him the salt, he thereby requests him to pass him the salt.

These rules — utterance meaning rules or 'pragmatic rules' — define utterance meanings. John Searle has called them 'constitutive rules';[121] J.L. Austin investigated them, for explicit performative utterances, in his doctrine of 'infelicities' (A1 − B2).[122] Other rules of this type would concern utterance synonymity or utterance entailment ('Whoever requests of $A$ that he do $U$ and $V$, thereby requests of him that he do $U$').

Then come the rules which $\Lambda$ consists of, for instance, as a part of $(\eta)$:

If $S$ is interested in $A$'s doing $V$ and if $A$ can do $V$, then if $S$ requests $A$ to do $V$, $A$'s obligation to do $V$ is increased.

Obligations begin to enter into the picture: 'real' rules greet from afar. But we should recall that the rules in $\Lambda$ may be only indirectly connected with obligations — for instance those which define an increase in responsibility.

The $\Lambda$ rules, together with pragmatic rules, entail rules of the following kind (*again a wrong example*):

If the speaker is standardly interested in the addressee's passing him the salt and if the addressee is normally able to pass it, then if the speaker utters a sentence with the sentence meaning that the addressee

---

121) *Speech Acts*, 2.5. In 2.7, Searle contrasts constitutive rules with 'regulative rules' in a somewhat misleading manner. I have tried to correct his exposition, while saving the basic ideas, in my paper, 'Some Elements of the Form of a Theory Perhaps Useful in Describing a Language'. See esp. pp. 91 − 95.

122) Under A1 − B2, Austin collected what is necessary for an (explicit) illocutionary act to be brought about by an utterance.

passes him the salt, the addressee's obligation to pass the speaker the salt is increased.

(We might, of course, refer to an utterance of 'Pass me the salt, please', instead.) Still, these are no direct rules about what to do. Let us now introduce the background conventions, considering two alternative ones. The first is prosocial, and leaving niceties aside, may state that if you can help somebody without great effort, a small obligation is sufficient for obligating you. We then have a convention the emergence of which in a system of conventions signals that some language is at work:

> If the speaker is standardly interested in the addressee's passing him the salt and if the addressee is normally able to pass it, then if the speaker utters 'Pass me the salt, please', the addressee has to pass him the salt.

This is a full—blooded, action—guiding rule. We might call it a linguistic convention because it describes a standard deviation from the background coventions explaining which forces us to impute the use of a conventional language to the group in question. — Now consider a more egotistical background convention which, leaving niceties aside, may state that if somebody can help himself, other people's obligations to come to his assistance are to be counterbalanced against his own obligation to take care of himself. According to this and supplementary background conventions, an alternative linguistic convention may look like this:

> If the speaker is standardly interested in the addressee's passing him the salt and if the addressee is normally able to pass ist, then if the speaker utters 'Pass me the salt, please', the obligation of the addressee to pass him the salt depends on whether or not the speaker can get to the salt himself, has to incommodate others in doing so, is socially superior to the addressee, ... etc.

This convention is also a linguistic one — for the same reason as in the above example —; however, it will not yield action—guiding rules unless further conventional facts obtain.

All of the above sentences are (in the context of, e.g., some linguistic inquiry) straightforwardly empirical in content. The last—mentioned, or lowest level ones inform us about the existence of rules in Hart's sense (or come close to such information), i.e. about rules being implicitly complied with; the first—mentioned, or high level ones are part of a theory which is explanatory with regard to lower levels and therefore *empirical rather than normative*. If considered under a different aspect, they are, of course, *theoretical rather than empirical*. It is in this respect that Λ sentences are so very theoretical that they altogether cease to be empirical and become analytic. To the lowest level empirical sentences, there are normative counterparts, namely rules which are normatively affirmed by most group members if they are actually complied with (see § 10). There are no such normative counterparts to the theoretical sentences; e.g. there is no rule that a German must not say, "Milch mir Zucker". There are only hypothetical imperatives of the form: "If you want to utter a German sentence, do not utter 'Milch mir Zucker'."

Unless a reductionist, one will agree that the parts of the theory on different levels refer to different things. Some refer to conventional make—ups, some to utterance meanings, some to sentence meanings. The reductionist will claim that even the highest level parts refer, in an indirect way, to nothing but observable social behavior; though not believing his, the non—reductionist will grant that unless there were complex social behavior, there would be no reason to assume theoretical entities like meanings. There could be no meanings without complex social behavior; however, social behavior could not be that complex without there being meanings.

# Appendix I: NIVEAU zero described

NIVEAU zero comprises what can be said by way of honking one's horn or flashing one's beams. The background conventions to be stated below may well be only part of the relevant ones, being those which the conventional results of utterances act most directly upon.

Background conventions

(BC 1)  $x$ is driving in his right lane, while $y$ is driving in his left lane; then $x$ ranks before $y$

(BC 2)  $x$ is on a public road, while $y$ is not; then $x$ ranks before $y$

(BC 3)  $x$ is in flowing traffic, $y$ in stationary traffic; then $x$ ranks before $y$

(BC 4)  $x$ is driving forward, $y$ backward; then $x$ ranks before $y$

(BC 5)  $x$ is driving on a main road, $y$ on a side road; then $x$ ranks before $y$

(BC 6)  From the point of view of $y$, $x$ comes from the right; then $x$ ranks before $y$

(BC 7)  $x$ keeps his lane, $y$ changes his lane; then $x$ ranks before $y$

In cases where two rules have incompatible results, the rule with the lower number applies.

(BC 9)  The easier it is for $x$ to avoid impeding or endangering $y$ and the more $y$ would be impeded or endangered, the less $x$ is permitted to impede or endanger $y$.

(BC 10) Everyone is individually responsible for the consequences of his driving maneuvers insofar as these maneuvers are not imposed upon him by law or by the maneuvers of other drivers.

(BC 11) In which manner and direction someone drives is his own business, as long as it is not forbidden or prescribed by the Road Traffic Regulations.

(BC 12) If $x$ does something useful for $y$ or if $y$ does something to $x$'s disadvantage, $y$ is liable for compensating $x$.

(BC 13) Each $x$ is obligated to protect each $y$ from damage. How strong his obligation is depends on the following: How great the damage would be, how much $x$ could help, how small his costs would be, and how difficult it would be for $y$ to avoid the damage himself.

In what follows, $U$ and $V$ are behaviors of $x$ and $y$, respectively. Referred to are only behaviors which drivers have standard interests in. Which one of the drivers is interested in which behavior is clear from the context.

Utterance meaning explications from $\Lambda$

($\alpha$) (PC) By failing to do $U$, $x$ prevents $y$ from doing $V$, $x$ is more entitled to omit doing $U$ than $y$ is to do $V$. (UM) Now $x$ *insists* to $y$ on omitting $U$. Then (CR) $x$ has to omit $U$; $y$ has to omit $V$; and $x$ comes to share more responsibility than before for the consequences of $V$'s being left undone.

($\beta$) (PC) By failing to do $U$, $x$ prevents $y$ from doing $V$; $x$ has more claim to omit doing $U$ than $y$ does have to do $V$. (UM) Now $x$ *offers* $y$ to do $U$. Then (CR) for a certain interval, $x$ is obligated to do $U$ if $y$ does $V$ within this interval; and $x$ comes to share more responsibility than before for the consequences of $y$'s doing $V$.

($\gamma$) (PC) $x$ has offered $y$ to do $U$. (UM) Now $y$ *accepts x's offer* (within the crucial interval). Then (CR) $x$ is obligated to do $U$; $y$ is obligated to do $V$; $y$ comes to share more responsibility than before for the consequences of $x$'s doing $U$.

($\delta$) (PC) By failing to do $U$, $x$ prevents $y$ from doing $V$; $y$ has requested $x$ to do $U$. (UM) Now $x$ *grants y's request* to do $U$. Then (CR) $x$ has to do $U$; $y$ has to do $V$; and $x$ comes to share more responsibility than before for the consequences of $V$.

($\epsilon$) (PC) By failing to do $U$, $x$ prevents $y$ from doing $V$. $y$ has requested $x$ to do $U$. (UM) Now $x$ *turns down y's request* to do $U$. Then (CR) $x$ has to omit $V$; $y$ is no more permitted to do $V$ than he was before his request; and $x$ comes to share more responsibility than before for the consequences of $V$ being left undone.

($\zeta$) (PC) $x$ has offered $y$ to do $U$. (UM) Now $y$ *declines x's offer* (within the crucial interval). Then (CR) $x$ is permitted to omit $U$; $y$ is obligated to omit $V$; and $y$ comes to share more responsibility than before for the consequences of $x$'s omitting $U$.

($\eta$) (PC) By failing to do $V$, $y$ prevents $x$ from doing $U$. (UM) Now $x$ *requests* $y$ to do $V$. Then (CR) $y$ becomes more obligated to do $V$; if $y$ does $V$, $x$ then will share more responsibility than before for the consequences of $V$; and if $y$ does $V$, then $x$ becomes considerably more obligated than before to do $U$.

138

($\vartheta$) (PC) $x$ and $y$ both have a common interest in coordinating their actions either in way $W1$ or in way $W2$. (UM) Now $x$ *proposes* to $y$ that they choose $W1$. Then (CR) for a certain interval, $x$ is obligated not to hinder either $W1$ or $W2$; if, within this interval, $y$ engages in $W1$, $x$ becomes obligated to follow $W1$ too; within this given interval, $y$ is obligated to do one of the following: engage in $W1$; agree to the proposal; reject the proposal; popose choosing $W2$; and $x$ is more responsible than $y$ for the consequences of their choosing $W1$.

($\iota$) (PC) $x$ did $U$ which is useful for $y$. (UM) Now $y$ *thanks* $x$ for doing $U$. Then (CR) $y$ is less liable for compensation of $U$ to $x$ than before.

($\varkappa$) (PC) $y$ did $V$ which is disadvantageous to $x$. (UM) Now $y$ *apologizes* to $x$ for doing $V$. Then (CR) $y$ is less liable for compensation of $V$ to $x$ than before.

($\lambda$) (PC) $y$ apologized to $x$ for doing $V$/thanked $x$ for doing $U$. (UM) Now $x$ *accepts $y$'s apologies/thanks*. Then (CR) $y$ is no longer liable for compensation of $V/U$ to $x$.

($\mu$) (PC) $y$ did $V$ which is disadvantageous to $x$. (UM) Now $x$ *reproaches* $y$ for doing $V$. Then (CR) $y$ is less liable for compensating $V$ to $x$ than before.

($\nu$) (PC) $x$ reproached $y$ for doing $V$. (UM) Now $y$ *rejects $x$'s reproach*. Then (CR) $y$ must expect everybody (including himself) to tolerate $V$.

($\xi$) (UM) $x$ *warns $y$ unspecifically*. Then (CR) if $y$ suffers damage, $x$ is in no way responsible for the amount of damage which $y$ could have avoided if he had been on the alert; and at $x$'s expense, $y$ can rely on an impending danger.

($o$) (PC) $x$ does not know, but is interested in knowing, if $p$ is the case, whereas $y$ knows it. (UM) Now $y$ *informs $x$ that $p$*. Then (CR) $x$ can rely at the expense of $y$ on $p$'s being the case.

Note that ($\xi$) lacks a precondition; this one is, therefore, our only general explication of an utterance meaning. − In ($o$), as in all explications of, and rules for utterance meanings, any empirical condition is to be construed as obtaining whenever it is expected to be obtaining by drivers' standards.

Utterance meaning rules of NIVEAU zero

(1)  By failing to do *U*, *x* prevents *y* from doing *V*; *x* is more entiteld to omit doing *U* than *y* is to do *V*. *x* signals and does something which is unsuitable for *y*'s doing *V*. Thereby, *x* *insists* to *y* on his omitting *V*.

(2)  By failing to do *U*, *x* prevents *y* from doing *V*; *x* has more claim to omit doing *U* than *y* does have to do *V*. *x* signals and does something which is suitable for *U*. Thereby, he *offers* *y* to do *U*.

(3)  *y* has offered *x* to do *V*. *x* signals and does something which is suitable for his taking advantage of the offer. He thereby *accepts* *y's offer* to do *V*.

(4)  *y* has offered *x* to do *V*. *x* signals and does something which is unsuitable for his taking advantage of the offer. Thereby, he *declines y's offer* to do *V*.

(5)  By failing to do *V*, *y* prevents *x* from doing *U*. *x* signals; thereby, he *requests* of *y* that he do *V*.

(6)  *y* has requested of *x* that he do *U*. *x* signals and does something which is unsuitable for *U*. Thereby, he *turns down y's request* that he do *U*.

(7)  *y* has requested of *x* that he do *U*. *x* signals and does something which is suitable for *U*. Thereby, he *grants y's request* that he do *U*.

(8)  *x* and *y* must coordinate their maneuvers either in way *W1* or in way *W2*. Neither has more claim than the other for choosing *W1* or *W2*. *x* signals and does something which is suitable for *W1* or unsuitable for *W2*; he thereby *proposes* to *y* that they both choose *W1*.

(9)  *x* did *U* which is useful for *y* with respect to driving quickly and/or safely. *y* signals; he thereby *thanks* *x* for doing *U*.

(10) *x* did *U* which is unfair to *y* with respect to driving quickly and/or safely. *x* signals; he thereby *apologizes* to *y* for doing *U*.

('Useful' and 'unfair' according to the group's standards, of course.)

(11) *y* apologized to *x* for doing *V*/thanked *x* for doing *U*; *x* signals. He thereby *accepts y's apologies/thanks*.

(12) *y* did *V* which is unfair to *x* with regard to driving quickly and/or safely; *x* signals. He thereby *reproaches y* for doing *V*.

(13) *x* reproached *y* for doing *V*; *y* signals. He thereby *rejects x's reproach*.

(14) *y* has an interest in obtaining the information, when it is the case that *p*. The information is available to *x*. *x* signals; he thereby *informs y* that it is the case that *p* at the time of signalling.

(17) *x* signals; no other rule applies. *x* thereby *warns y unspecifically*.

The corresponding rule (17) of NIVEAU − see Appendix II − also refers back to the other rules, and I preferred to make it the last one. Rules (15) and (16) of NIVEAU have no counterparts in NIVEAU zero; this explains the lacuna between (14) and 17).

# Appendix II: NIVEAU described

In the description of NIVEAU, additional *background conventions* are not taken care of. Some at least would have to be considered. The use of the blinkers would, for instance, be unintelligible unless there was a valid background convention to the effect that everybody has to stick to his direction, or at least that everybody else is entitled to rely on him to stick to it.

There is just one additional *utterance meaning explication*, viz. for asking yes − no questions. Although these can be asked by use of horn or headlight flash as well as, for instance, by pointing, it is no good reckoning them with NIVEAU zero, because answers can be given only in NIVEAU (see § 32).

($\pi$) (PC) *x* does not know, but is interested in learning whether or not it is the case that *p*. (UM) Now *x asks y whether or not it is the case that p*. Then (CR) if *y* knows whether or not *p* he is more obligated than before to inform *x* whether or not *p*.

The semantics

| *Signs* | *sm attributions to signs* |
|---|---|
| direction gesture | that *A* moves in the direction indicated |
| pointing gesture | |
| (a) directed at *A* or *A*'s car: | *A* or *A*'s car, respectively |
| (b) not directed at *A*'s car: | that *S* drives in the direction indicated |
| beckoning gesture | that *A* approaches *S* |
| distance marking gesture | that the distance is such as indicated |
| wheel turning gesture | that *A* turns the wheel in the direction indicated |

| | |
|---|---|
| slowing down gesture | that $A$ slows down |
| thanking gesture | - - - |
| nodding, holding one's thumb up | |
| (a) no preceding utterance directed at $S$: | that what $A$ is interested in is the case |
| (b) preceding utterance directed at $S$: | that the preceding utterance's meaning's proposition is the case |
| shaking one's head, waving one's hand in a certain way | |
| (a) no preceding utterance directed at $S$: | that what $A$ is interested in is not the case |
| (b) preceding utterance directed at $S$: | that the preceding utterance's meaning's proposition is not the case |
| right/left blinker | |
| (a) a move to the right/left is feasible: | that $S$ intends to move to the right/left |
| (b) no move to the right/left is feasible: | that $S$ does not intend to move to the left/right |
| beam flashing | - - - |
| horn honking | - - - |
| blue flashing light, police sirene | that $A$ keeps away from $S$ |
| warning blinker (including flashing orange light) | that $S$ is an obstacle |
| warning triangle | that there is danger ahead of $A$ |
| driving maneuver which is a performance of $M$ | that $S$ intends $M$ |

*Warning*: Treating the thanking gesture exactly like horn and headlight flash is empirically incorrect. In this respect, the description of NIVEAU wants correction.

Utterance meaning rules

The following abbreviation will be used:

For 'x uses a sign without an *sm* and does something which ..., or $x$ uses a sign with an *sm* which ...', we write: '$x$ uses a sign and *sm* − replaceably does something which ...'.

Reference to collision of interests is omitted for the sake of brevity.

(1)  $x$ is more entitled to omit doing $U$ than $y$ is to claim that he do it. $x$ uses a sign and *sm* − replaceably does something which is unsuitable for $U$. He thereby *insists* on $x$'s omitting $U$.

(2) $x$ is more entitled to omit doing $U$ than $y$ is to claim that he do it. $x$ uses a sign and $sm$—replaceably does something which is suitable for $U$. He thereby *offers $y$ to do $U$.*

(3) $y$ has offered $x$ to do $V$. $x$ uses a sign and $sm$—replaceably does something which is suitable for his taking advantage of the offer. He thereby *accepts $y$'s offer* to do $V$.

(4) $y$ has offered $x$ to do $V$. $x$ uses a sign and $sm$—replaceably does something which is unsuitable for his taking advantage of the offer. He thereby *declines $y$'s offer* to do $V$.

(5) $x$ uses a sign without an $sm$, or he uses a sign with an $sm$ which is either suitable for $y$'s doing $V$ or a possible motive for $x$'s interest in $y$ doing $V$. $x$ thereby *requests* of $y$ that he do $V$.

(6) $y$ has requested of $x$ that he do $U$. $x$ uses a sign and $sm$—replaceably does something which is unsuitable for $U$. He thereby *turns down $y$'s request* that he do $U$.

(7) $y$ has requested of $x$ that he do $U$. $x$ uses a sign and $sm$—replaceably does something which is suitable for $U$. He thereby *grants $y$'s request* that he do $U$.

(8) $x$ and $y$ must coordinate their maneuvers either in way $W1$ or in way $W2$. Neither is more entitled than the other to choose either way. $x$ uses a sign and $sm$—replaceably does something which is suitable for $W1$ or unsuitable for $W2$; he thereby *proposes* to $y$ that they choose $W1$.

(9) $y$ did $V$ which was useful for $x$ with respect to driving quickly and/or safely. $x$ uses a sign without an $sm$. He thereby *thanks $y$* for doing $V$.

(10) $x$ did $U$ which was unfair to $y$ with respect to driving quickly and/or safely. $x$ uses a sign without an $sm$. He thereby *apologizes* to $y$ for doing $U$.

(11) $y$ apologized to $x$ for doing $V$/thanked $x$ for doing $U$. $x$ uses a sign without an $sm$. He thereby *accepts $y$'s apologies/thanks.*

(12) $y$ did $V$ which was unfair to $x$ with respect to driving quickly and/or safely. $x$ uses a sign without an $sm$. He thereby *reproaches $y$* for doing $V$.

(13) $y$ reproached $x$ for doing $U$. $x$ uses a sign without an $sm$. He thereby *rejects $y$'s reproach.*

(14) $y$ has an interest in obtaining the information when it is the case that $p$. The information is available to $x$. $x$ uses a sign without an $sm$. He thereby *informs $y$ that at the time of the utterance it is the case that $p$.*

(15)  *x* has an interest in knowing whether or not it is the case that *p*. *y* knows whether or not it is the case that *p*. *x* uses a sign whose *sm* — if any — is the reference of *p*. He thereby *asks y whether or not it is the case that p.*

(16)  *y* has an interest in doing *V*; however, he does not know whether or not he may do *V*. *x* knows whether or not *y* may do *V*.

(i)   *x* uses a sign whose *sm* lawfully implies that *y* may (must not) do *V*. He thereby *informs y that he may (must not) do V.*

(ii)   *x* uses a sign whose *sm* is the contradictory of an (i) — sign's *sm*. He thereby *informs y that he must not (may) do V.*

(17)  No other rule applies.

(i)   *x* uses a sign whose *sm* is that *A* does *V*. He thereby *requests* of *y* that *y* do *V*.

(ii)   *x* uses a sign whose *sm* is that *p* (for some *p* other than that *y* does *V*). He thereby *informs y that p.*

(iii)   *x* uses a sign which is missing a 'that *p*' *sm*. He thereby *warns y unspecifically.* (If the *sm* is some thing, then the warning refers to this thing.)

The circumstances where (17) intervenes do not suffice for the preconditions of ($\eta$) — requesting —, or ($o$) — informing — to hold. Thus the explanation of conventional deviations is not complete. I suggested a missing link in my *Zum Begriff der Sprache*, § 83. The general idea is: Where utterance meanings can be generated in situations where their $\Lambda$ preconditions are not satisfied, the speaker is less dependent on circumstances. *For more ease* in speaking, *he pays by taking the responsibility* for the $\Lambda$ preconditions to obtain. The idea is confirmed by the fact that some plausible conversational implicatures can be derived from it.

Bibliography

William P. Alston, *Philosophy of Language*, Englewood Cliffs, N.J., (Prentice — Hall), 1964

John L. Austin, *How to Do Things with Words*, Oxford, (Oxford University Press), [2]1975

Kent Bach, Robert M. Harnish, *Linguistic Communication and Speech Acts*, Cambridge, Mass., (M.I.T. Press), 1979

Gordon P. Baker, 'Defeasability and Meaning', in: Peter M.S. Hacker and Joseph Raz eds., *Law, Morality, and Society*, Oxford, (Clarendon Press), 1977, 26 — 57

Jonathan Bennett, 'The Meaning — Nominalist Strategy', *Foundations of Language* 10, 1973, 141 — 168

— — — *Linguistic Behaviour*, Cambridge, (Cambridge University Press), 1976

John Biro, 'Conventionality in Speech Acts', *Southwest Philosophical Studies*, 1978, 11 — 17

— — — 'Intentionalism in the Theory of Meaning', *The Monist*, 62, 1979, 238 — 258

— — — 'Conditions for Phatic Acts: A Non — Mentalistic Analysis', in: *Sprache, Logik und Philosophie* (4. Internationaler Wittgenstein — Kongreß), Wien, (Hoelder — Pichler — Tempsky), 1980, 429 — 433

Robert Brandom, 'Asserting', *Nous* 17, 1983, 637 — 650

Tyler Burge, 'On Knowledge and Convention', *Philosophical Review* 84, 1975, 249 — 255

L. Jonathan Cohen, 'Do Illocutionary Forces Exist?', *Philosophical Quarterly* 14, 1964, 118 — 137

David E. Cooper, 'Meaning and Illocutions', *American Philosophical Quarterly* 9, 1972, 69 — 77

— — — 'Lewis on Our Knowledge of Conventions', *Mind* 86, 1977, 255 — 261

Donald Davidson, 'Reality without Reference', *Dialectica* 31, 1977, 247 — 258

Roger Doorbar, 'Meaning, Rules, and Behaviour', *Mind* 80, 1971, 29 — 40

Ronald M. Dworkin, 'Social Rules and Legal Theory', *The Yale Law Journal* 81, 1972, 855 — 890; = chapter III from: *Taking Rights Seriously*, Cambridge, Mass., (Harvard University Press), 1978

Margret Gilbert, 'Agreements, Conventions, and Language', *Synthese* 54, 1983, 375 — 407

Günther Grewendorf, 'Explizit performative Äußerungen und Feststellungen', in: id. ed., *Sprechakttheorie und Semantik*, Frankfurt a. M., (Suhrkamp), 1979, 197–216

H. Paul Grice, 'Meaning', *Philosophical Review* 66, 1957, 377–388

– – –'Utterer's Meaning, Sentence Meaning, and Word Meaning', *Foundations of Language* 4, 1968, 225–242

– – –'Utterer's Meaning and Intentions', *Philosophical Review* 78, 1969, 147–177

– – –'Meaning Revisited', in: N.V. Smith ed., *Mutual Knowledge*, New York (Academic Press), 1982, 223–243

Peter M.S. Hacker, 'Sanction Theories of Duty', in: Alfred W.B. Simpson ed., *Oxford Essays in Jurisprudence*, Oxford (Clarendon Press), 1973, 131–170

– – –'Hart's Philosophy of Law', in: Peter M.S. Hacker and Joseph Raz eds., *Law, Morality and Society*, Oxford (Clarendon Press), 1977, 1–25

Herbert L.A. Hart, *The Concept of Law*, Oxford (Clarendon Press), 1961

Irene Heim, *Zum Verhältnis von Wahrheitsbedingungen–Semantik und Sprechakttheorie*, Proc. of the Sonderforschungsbereich 99, Universität Konstanz, 1977

Carl G. Hempel, 'The Theoretician's Dilemma', in: Carl G. Hempel, *Aspects of Scientific Explanation*, New York (The Free Press) and London (Collier–Macmillan), 1968, 173–226

David Holdcroft, 'Meaning and Illocutionary Acts', *Ratio* 6, 1964, 128–143

Dale Jamieson, 'David Lewis on Convention', *Canadian Journal of Philosophy* 5, 1975, 73–81

Andrew Jones, *Communication and Meaning*, Dordrecht (Reidel) 1983 (Synthese Library, Vol. 168)

Andreas Kemmerling, *Konvention und sprachliche Kommunikation*, Dissertation München 1976

– – –'Was Grice mit "Meinen" meint', in: Günther Grewendorf ed., *Sprechakttheorie und Semantik*, Frankfurt a. M. (Suhrkamp), 1979, 67–118

– – –'Utterer's Meaning Revisited', in: Richard Grandy, Richard Warner eds., *Philosophical Grounds of Rationality: Intentions, Categories, Ends*, Oxford (Clarendon Press), 1986, 131–155.

David K. Lewis, *Convention*, Cambridge, Mass. (Harvard University Press), 1969

– – –'Languages and Language', in: K. Gunderson ed., *Language,*

*Mind, and Knowledge* (Minnesota Studies in the Philosophy of Science VII), Minneapolis, Minnesota (University of Minnesota Press), 1975, 3−35

− − −'Convention: Reply to Jamieson', *Canadian Journal of Philosophy* 6, 1976, 113−120

Brian Loar, 'Two Theories of Meaning', in: G. Evans, J. McDowell eds., *Truth and Meaning*, Oxford (Oxford University Press) 1976, 138−161

David Lumsden, 'Does Speaker's Reference Have Semantic Relevance?', *Philosophical Studies* 47, 1985, 15−21

William L. McBride, 'The Acceptance of a Legal System', *The Monist* 49, 1965, 377−396

Georg Meggle, *Grundbegriffe der Kommunikation*, Berlin (de Gruyter) 1981

Herbert Morris, 'Hart's Concept of Law', *Harvard Law Review* 75, 1962, 1452−1461

B.C. O'Neill, 'Conventions and Illocutionary Force', *Philosophical Quarterly* 22, 1972, 215−233

Joseph Raz, *Practical Reason and Norms*, London (Hutchinson), 1975

Eike von Savigny, *Die Philosophie der normalen Sprache*, completely revised edition, Frankfurt a. M. (Suhrkamp), 1974

− − −'Some Elements of The Form of an Theory Perhaps Useful in Describing a Language', in: Gilbert Ryle ed., *Contemporary Aspects of Philosophy*, Stocksfield 1976, 86−102

− − −'Listener−Oriented Versus Speaker−Oriented Analysis of Conventional Meaning', *American Philosophical Quarterly* 13, 1976, 69−74

− − −'Das normative Fundament der Sprache: Ja und Aber', *Grazer Philosophische Studien* 2, 1977, 141−158

− − − *Die Signalsprache der Autofahrer*, München (Deutscher Taschenbuch Verlag), 1980

− − − *Zum Begriff der Sprache*, Stuttgart (Reclam), 1983

Stephen Schiffer, *Meaning*, Oxford (Clarendon Press), 1972

John R. Searle, *Speech Acts*, Cambridge (Cambridge University Press), 1969

Marcus G. Singer, 'Hart's Concept of Law', *The Journal of Philosophy* 60, 1963, 197−220

Robert S. Stalnaker, 'Assertion', in: Peter Cole ed., *Syntax and Semantics, Vol. 9: Pragmatics*, New York (Academic Press), 1978, 315−332

Peter F. Strawson, 'Intention and Convention in Speech Acts', *Philosophical Review* 73, 1964, 439 – 460

Geoffrey J. Warnock, *The Object of Morality*, London (Methuen), 1971

Ludwig Wittgenstein, *Philosophical Investigations*, Oxford (Blackwell), 1953, 3rd ed. 1967

# Subject Index

(Numerals refer to sections.)